An Upland Place

An Upland Place

Further writings from

Elizabeth Macpherson

Illustrated by
Joanne Yeadon

Librario

Published by

Librario Publishing Ltd.

ISBN 10 : 1-904440-90-8
ISBN 13 : 978-1904440901

Copies can be ordered from retail
or via the internet at:
www.librario.com

or from:

Brough House
Milton Brodie
Kinloss
Moray
IV36 2UA
Tel / Fax: 01343 850178

Printed in Times.

Cover design and typesetting by Steven James
www.chimeracreations.co.uk

Printed and bound by
Digital Quill, Edinburgh Scotland
www.digiquill.co.uk

The Year's First Snow

It is snowing as I write, the year's first snow. For weeks now we have been watching winter's victories over the high empires of the far hills, and daily the triumphant armies have marched ever nearer.

Last night we discovered them at our gates, for when we went to make the goodnight round of the beasts cold sleety showers obliterated the stars and sent the fugitive moon careening over the dark moor. We shivered as we smelt the ice in the wind, and to-day has fulfilled the weather's portents. The snow is here.

We live in a strange, small world alone. Thick mist, obscure as Styx, has closed in on us.

The wide horizons of our familiar everyday world are vanished, and instead we inhabit a new universe, intimate, significant, and transmuted.

Here is the home of quiet. Silent flake follows silent flake, multitudinous and lovely as the prayers of the blessed. There is nothing whatsoever in this shut-in place of our dwelling that does not cherish the benison of the snow.

The long withered pluff grass, remembering dead beauty, once more rears its plumes in the air, but where they were green and rosy lavender now they are silver. The garden fence, once netting wire, is now frail lace, and the curled black satin of burst broom pods wears a cluster of snow blossoms over its empty heart.

The larches behind the house have at last forgotten their golden needles, for their boughs are no longer barren but bear a new foliage, thick, argent, dreaming.

The steading roofs are white save where the byre is placed, and there a dark patch appears for the warm breath of the cows has melted the snow from the slates.

The beasts are all inside and the hens have all gone to roost except one stray white Wyandotte, who, with her shining feathers and coral comb, looks as if she would be more at home in a Chinese print than wandering in the Scottish hills.

Duck also is abroad performing a Spartan toilet in a snow-encrusted puddle. Drake, wrapt in wondering admiration, regards her with his head on one side.

I open the window to have a word with them, and the air strikes, purged, clean, and invigorating on my face.

The gauds, the passions and anxieties that make up the life blood of the human year suddenly are not. The white world, blest and absolved, defies the gathering dark.

By Burn and River

Our two farms are girdled by water. At home our fields all slope down towards the burn which ambles meditatively between its ragged banks of peat. It is a very small burn, and I am afraid that except to the eyes of our love it isn't a very impressive or beautiful one.

Poor thing, it hasn't even a pretty name, but wears its un-euphonious Cnockack with unpretending carelessness. It rises somewhere out on the moor, and after a sluggish, sluttish start amid bogs and acid wells arrives yawning at the foot of the corn park.

Here it begins to perk up its notions. It makes a breenge at the fence, and proceeds to dance round little gravel islands and insinuate itself under rough banks overgrown with rank heather. Soon it comes to the foot of the place we call the Towm, and at once breaks into flowery meads where marsh marigold and violets contend to mirror themselves within its brown shallows.

A thicket of birch oversown with windflowers invites its small water. Wild duck with their families play in its wider pools, and an occasional homeless otter leaves its doglike marks on its little sandy coves.

Once past the wood the Cnockack forgets its drab beginnings, and as if conscious that it must soon lose its identity in the larger Dorback (which comes to meet it), it adorns itself with bank upon bank of memliss, so that to the casual eye it ceases to be a burn and becomes instead a cascade of gold.

And so at last it reaches journey's end in the embrace of the big river which all this time has been hurrying to engulf it.

The Dorback comes all the way out of bleak and desolate Dava, rushing and tearing its way through gravelly sandy banks. It is wild and impetuous until it reaches our quieter ways, where birch and alder grow.

At the other farm it enters a wide, deep gorge, which is so gentle and sheltered that even in roughest winter beasts may lie here secure. Craigs of sand and rock shut out all save the most sighing airs. In this quiet place one may leave winter behind, and in storm may dream of summer days.

In spring and right on throughout the year wide green meadows stretch out beguiling arms to the caressing air. There is no lovelier end to a summer day than to come here and see the summering beasts couched amid juniper and broom. Air and light are muted in this tranquil place, and the river whispers to the spiralling gnats as if hushed with it own peace.

Round the corner, where boulders bar the way, the two waters of the farms meet and together pass from our land. Farther than we can see or hear they rush towards a deep waterfall, but that is beyond our ken. We enjoy and give thanks for what lies at home, and within ourselves find our own solace.

The Wintering Sheep

Winter in the mountain sheep farms of Scotland is so rigorous that the farmers there cannot hope to carry all their flocks through its storms and starvations. Instead, they are compelled to send the majority of their stock down to the lower country, where there is more shelter and where the grazings are more hospitable.

For the past fortnight our roads have been busy with the traffic this entails. Float after float filled to treble decker capacity labours carefully down from Dava to the lower reaches of Moray.

As I watch the endless procession I cannot help marvelling at the revolution wrought by the motor engine in the aspect and economy of the countryside.

In the old days such wintering sheep were walked to their destination by the drovers, those gipsies of pastoral farming, who walked with their flocks and herds from Corryarick to Falkirk Tryst, from Falkirk back to their mountain fastnesses, and from there again all over Scotland and into England.

They saw the world, or, at least, a wild, ebullient part of it.

All day they travelled on foot behind their leisurely charges, and at evening supped off "cold steer," that is oatmeal mixed with cold water. What if they did illumine such fare with copious draughts of whisky?

When night came, and all its stars, they wrapped themselves in their plaids and slept in the open, with their beasts beside them. It was a hard, adventurous, and picturesque life; but there is no place for it on our bustling highways to-day.

The drovers have gone, but here and there throughout the Highlands are open spaces near the roadways which the few remaining inhabitants call the "Stance."

In such places the drovers rested their tired flocks and themselves spent the night companioned by the dumb beasts and the lofty elements.

The change from the drover to the motor bus is economic and humane, for the sheep do not now have to make the long, tiring journeys, which reduced their condition very badly.

Yet it seems a poor exchange for the mere spectator to see, instead of a picturesque Highlander proud with the romance of his journeying, an old Roman-nosed yowe complacently admiring autumn's lovely gold from the top deck of a double-decker float.

Doom and Reprieve?

For some weeks now we have been finding the capricious dominion of our tame sheep Christina more and more intolerable.

It was bad enough when she insisted on accompanying us about the farm and going for walks with us, on which she took care to exhibit to the passers-by our least dignified aspects. But she found these methods of infuriation lose their piquancy, and in the wickedness of her grey-domed head she worked out a new set of plans for our discomfiture.

First she took to refusing her legitimate neeps, but waited like a reiver till the neep-shed door opened, and then she flew in, in front of you. Before you got back your angry breath there she was gobbling down turnips to a band playing.

With difficulty you drove her out, and then she made straight for the barn and dived in at the lower half of the door.

Now you must know that at the barn door there is a little trough filled with bruised corn and flaked maize specially for Christina. But does she look at it and think with gratitude that she is not in starving Europe? She does not.

She attacks instead with most unsheeplike gusto the bag of calf nuts and the treacle barrel, which are both inside the barn.

Blows and Bellows

Just to point her insolence she skilfully upsets forks, bin lids, and riddles as she makes her breenge for the forbidden fruit, the horrid woolly Eve. Being human we fall on her with blows and bellows, which, owing to the thickness of her coat, have but a muffled effect.

At last, when she has eaten her malicious fill, she turns an inquiring topaz eye upon us, as who should say "Did you speak? I thought, perhaps, maybe . . . "

Well, we bore all this with grim and growing anger, and then the snow came, to be succeeded by thaw, which promptly became ice.

Christina, taking counsel with the witches, waited till she met a human with a pail of milk crossing the icy plain, and then she made a bright and girlish lunge.

I could stand no more. I came home and telephoned the mart to see would they take a fat sheep? They would, but here's the rub. They wouldn't take her for a fortnight. Well, I figured we could just hold out.

What do you think Christina has done now? Gone all charming.

She picks up her worsted petticoats, and, dancing, partners winter in the snowy fields; she gambols at the tractor wheels like any innocent love, and makes entrancing gestures at the children's swing.

If I'm not a poor, bewitched, weak-minded woman.

No House for the Ducks

Last night I peered through a window still unseasonably glacéd by frost at a marbled world illuminated by a half-hearted moon. This spring's incessant warfare between thaw and not-thaw has resulted in the most comical landscape, where bands of dark, bare ground alternate with banks of purest snow so that by daylight the world looks as if some irresponsible giant had got tired of sucking his chocolate cream and had wiped his fingers on hill and moor.

At night, beneath the watery moon, the idle eye can amuse itself working out the significances of the black and white universe.

Tapestried animals and heraldic maps sprawl across the moors, and it is fun to read strange islands and valleys in the Dalmatian coloured hills. Sometimes your imaginings are woefully out as mine were last night.

I was just apprehending an archipelago in alabaster when suddenly the whole thing rose and waddled off towards the byre wall. It wasn't a fairy land forlorn at all I'd been looking at but the crescent of our dozen white Aylesbury ducks, who suddenly, having got tired of staring out the moon, decided by that simultaneous impulse, which on this farm moves all ducks but one, to seek a warmer resting place.

For the hundredth time my heart smote me and I said, "We'll have to build a duck house for the poor creatures."

The trouble about the ducks here is that we can't take them seriously. It's over 12 years now since old Duck, that riotous old piece, escaped the crate that was to take her and all her companions to market.

After her years of solitary virgin life we were kindly given a husband for her, and for a brief idyllic summer she remained in love. But her leering, cynical attitude to life reasserted itself and she soon reverted from the domesticity of hearth and home to the prodigal life more native to her.

In vain we pointed out the virtues and benefits of a decent matron's life, in vain her two virtuous daughters, who were the sole survivors of numerous mismanaged progeny, besought her for the sake of her grandchildren to turn from her hedonistic ways.

She laughed loud ha ha laughs and went off to wilder debauches than ever in the muddy meadows, and reeled home more raucously than before beneath the wondering moon.

How could we build a house for an abandoned female like that? I ask you! Could you bring yourself to work with nails and wood and foot rules to make a hearth for someone who would regard you with a lickerish bright eye?

I have no wish to be made to feel futile, so the ducks' house remains a pious aspiration. How sad, too, that all the other virtuous ducks should suffer rheumatics all because of their outrageous grandma.

They say, though, "Virtue is its own reward." Indeed, I truly hope so.

Joe, the Farmhand
from Nowhere

The legal authorities are still busy trying to tidy up Joe's affairs. The search for documents and relatives which led from Hamburg to Vienna seems to have got swamped in the Danube and I doubt if we'll ever discover whether Joe Albrecht's ancient aunt still survives somewhere in Middle Europe, or whether his mother confided his father's name to any record office this side of Budapest.

Joe first came to our farm 13 years ago when farm labour was very difficult and there was a camp of German ex-P.O.W.s down the road. These men for one reason or another wished to stay in this country and Joe was one of them. I shall not forget my first sight of this tall burly fellow standing on my kitchen doorstep in the dark of a back end which was frosty and bleak. His eyes glittered under a large black cloth cap and his right hand was encased in plaster which he explained he had come by because he'd had a fight with another compatriot and in thrashing his opponent he'd broken his thumb.

* * *

This information I found sadly unreassuring but the fact of a byreful of in-calf heifers needing attention made us think that perhaps we better swallow our misgivings. I doubt really if we'd have had much say in the matter for Joe had already made up his mind to come.

There was on old tumbledown cottage which he annexed for his home since he had no intention of paying me the statutory fee for board and lodging. He had come to make money, he said, and make it he did. Because he realized that all overtime pay would have been subject to income tax, he worked out an ingenious table by which he was paid in kind instead of money. By judicious juggling with perquisites he was able to save practically all his wage and he kept his wealth in a hole under the disused hearth.

Now and again he would come all over suspicious and we'd have to rush down to Forres to buy a new lock for his door because he swore someone had taken the impression of the key of the existing one. We found it all a great strain but he worked like a mad thing and we were reluctant to deal more firmly with him.

Then he took to gardening and at night he used to labour on through the dark, building sheltering walls and digging and trenching the old weedy garden behind his cottage. With the spring he grew huge vegetables which he sold and still his money grew.

When he considered us it was with contempt. We had neither skill nor knowledge; and fancy calling in a vet when a tisane of camomile flowers would heal any cow in the fold. Fools – that's what we were. In Germany things were different.

Finally we got that we could not bear Joe another minute though we respected him as a force of nature, and we passed him on to a friend who accepted him as such.

Unhappily our friend's other workers did not take quite the same view and our friend decided that Joe had better seek other horizons. Because the friend was wealthy and admiring he set Joe up in a croft and there the old tough went in for pig feeding and an intensive study of the bible.

He also took to letter writing which he taught himself out of an old text book he picked up somewhere. He certainly never bought it. On market days we used to see him in Elgin, grave, well-doing, and faintly smelling of stye. His sole concession to convention was to abandon his black cap and arrange for new specs on the National

Health. His old specs had been mended with snare wire and they gave his weather-beaten face a certain wild distinction.

Then quite suddenly he died. I had helped with his naturalisation papers but before the formalities were completed he was dead: a stateless person.

Varieties of Party Spirit

Because of my official capacity as local busy-body, I find myself involved during the week before Christmas in an orgy of country school parties.

In the school in the forest above the Findhorn I am invited to Christmas dinner with carols by the pupils to aid post-prandial digestion. The largest of the three establishments in a parish which used to sustain six, asks me to meet Father Christmas and partake of tea and a "baggie," while the smallest seat of all extends its good wishes and hopes I can come and see the scholars play oranges and lemons before Santa comes to give them presents off their tinsellated tree.

* * *

Poor pets, regardless of the axe impending, they'll all be wearing their best clothes with ribbons in their hair and stars in their eyes. As I thank them for their thought I wonder if this will be the last party in the old school where not so long ago there were 60 pupils; and scholars who were destined to be famous men of learning in ancient Scottish universities learned their A B C between these four walls.

All three parties are as different in character as they can be, which argues a wonderful residuum of individuality in one depopulated upland parish. Yet they are sturdily rooted in a single stock – that ineradicable family feeling which is at once the strength and weakness of the Scottish character, since to it we owe our patriotism as well as our provincialism.

None of the schools could have any festivity at all if it were not for the parents who organize sales of works and whists and dances to pay for the affair. We do not aspire to Parents' and Teachers' Associations but our committees are powerful in their own right.

* * *

In a small community like ours, this means we pay levy several times over. For the Logie parents to attend a dance in the wooden shed which does hilarious duty for a village hall at Dava is but the decent *quid pro quo* for the masses of raffle tickets the Davadonians bought to augment the Logie exchequer.

This beautiful one-ness of heart is not expected to last throughout the year and Dava would consider itself lacking in civic sense if it kept quiet about the way some folk in the glen run the village activities. Similarly there are plenty people not in Dava who feel justified in harbouring very dark suspicions about who owns some of the sheep who stravaig the wild moor. Like a wider world we acknowledge the common denominator of our humanity once a year only.

But school parties are not only for the pupils. They are for their parents, too. Mothers who cannot attend Rural or Guild make the supreme effort to come to the school party. They bring all their children, toddlers, and babies in arms. Later, fathers will arrange to collect the lot, family, Moses baskets, and the remains of the tea baggies, not to mention the presents from the Christmas tree.

The row in the village hall is strident and deafening. I have never ceased to be impressed by the placidity of mothers gossiping tranquilly while their off-spring tear the place apart. Some run rackety races from platform to door and others fight to the death and the effusion of blood. Over all there is the strong hearty smell of tea a-boil in the urn in the kitchen.

Then miraculously silence falls and the children who have been giving a fair imitation of fiends at play gather round the teacher, and as their thin sweet voices rise in the angelic treble of "Away in a Manger" the significance of the occasion shines out like a star.

Snowploughs to
the Rescue

We are becoming quite up-to-date about snowstorms here, and come another year or another blizzard we'll be as nonchalant about its inconveniences as the advertisers – announcing snowploughs as the coming wear for tractors in the New Year – insist.

We certainly have progressed enormously in the road clearing business in the last 10 years. I remember when the road from Forres to Grantown would be blocked for days on end and when a snowplough did eventually turn up from Elgin down in the Laich, it wore a surprised and pained expression just as if it had caught Dava moor out in some bucolic solecism. Snow wreaths we were given to understand were definitely Non-U.

However we have now got it over that we do not arrange snowstorms just to be difficult and the pundits automatically arrange for our roads to be kept open without our distraught appeals. They even sand our wildest gradients of their own volition.

But farms for the most part are not situated bang on the Queen's highway so that even when through-traffic is proceeding on its perilous one way, we remain immured each on our own private ice-floe.

It is now that the tractor-mounted snowplough comes into its triumphant own. The old home-made timber affair drawn by horses and weighted down with granite boulders has long since mouldered away beneath the smitten larch, but the new one ramps round the house and steading in a flourish of efficiency and no time at all.

* * *

One needs so many paths about a farm. Most important, of course, is the access road which brings you the post and the vet, the baker and the cattle float. One year our access road, although the shortest one in the parish, remained blocked for a fortnight and we had to take to the fields to find our way out. In the end we got the loan of a neighbour's dung-loader to howk through the worst of the drifts.

But though the access road is important it is not the one we use most. Our most beaten track is the one that leads from the house to the steading, and it carries all the drudgery of the incessant day. Hay in bales carried from Nissen hut to fold goes this way, and so does the enamel pudding dish of porridge for the cats in the barn, who are dreadfully ill-used since yesterday's hot meal froze before they had finished it. The electric kettle finds itself a park on this path. It was carried out full of hot water to help melt the drinking fountains in the byre and has been forgotten by the angry amateur plumber.

* * *

With the beasts needing such a lot of attention the domestic difficulties of the house get overlooked, and I sigh for a neat little road to be cut for me to the clothes rope and the dump in the wood. There is, too, the small matter of a path to the coal cellar; but, after all, I can manage thus far in my Wellington boots, and with a handy shovel can cut a passage that will ensure that I do not get snow down my boot legs to melt uncomfortably against my stockings.

Smiler the cat accompanies me on this undertaking. As the snow flies dry and powdery from the shovel she chases it imagining it a flight of birds. They, poor things, sit brooding on the sloping roof of the old garage beseeching me for largesse. Once the cat is safely asleep beside the hearth they get their food and their water.

Out on the hill the wintering sheep announce themselves independent of either county snowplough or tractor-mounted farm affair. They have effected a hard-packed trail leading from moor to the place where they are fed their hay and make their slow sure way there morning and night.

Farewell to the "Marginal"

We have just completed the filling in of what must be our last "marginal" form of all time, and therefore we have the empty, swept, and garnished feeling which comes of being present at the end of a historic epoch.

For upland farming the Marginal Aid Production Grant, introduced as a war-time measure, turned out to be as revolutionary an innovation as the introduction of the turnip and crop rotation, for it demonstrated in startling fashion to the man working acres lacking the advantages of climate and recuperative quality what could be grown with artificial manure (sack muck).

Hitherto all the fertiliser used on these inhospitable places had been farmyard manure and this was for ever in short supply, for the scanty crops it grew meant the fewer beasts kept and the fewer beasts the less manure.

* * *

As a matter of interest we went through the valuations paid on this place when the tenancy was taken over two years before the war began. The only cereal grown was oats and they were valued at three quarters to the acre for ley, and half of that for the clean land. By the end of the war barley was as easily grown as oats, potatoes for seed had become a common-place crop, and the yields for grain crops were running at somewhere between six quarters for barley and as much as 10 for oats per acre.

There is a mighty difference between three quarters and 10 quarters. Grass, which had never been really reckoned a crop, was now coming into its own and places which used to imagine that hay was not ready to cut till August found themselves with crops ready for the mower by the end of June. And the credit for this must in the first instance be given to the "marginal," though, since success begets success, farmers themselves soon began to exercise drive and imagination.

The way the grant was administered was simple enough. All farms lying above a certain altitude were surveyed and the percentage of aid was tied to the height above sea level. There were anomalies. Dairy farms in hill land were not eligible; nor were poor places lying near the coast. There were, too, rich upland farms with deep acres placed fortunately to the sun and they too got help along with their neighbours.

Every year the marginal farmer got a form on which to state his cropping plans for the coming season. He knew his own plans were not really invited but he did not object since he who pays the manure merchant can rightly call the crop. If he thought the amount of lime he was required to spread in excess of what his land needed, he kept his doubts to himself along with the receipts from his manure and grass-seed merchants.

One of the conditions about the "marginal" was that you got not one penny till you could show your receipts. To some farmers initially short of capital this was a sore point, but as matters improved financially less and less was heard about the so-and-so's in the office who were sticky about paying out.

War-time conditions gradually eased and the need for cereal cropping became less urgent. First oats got difficult to sell and then barley, and farmers were asked to use them on the farm for feeding beasts. Grassland took on a new look and the silage pit replaced the cornyard. "Marginal" with its rigid conditions suitable for a siege economy found itself out of date. But its memory will long be green with us in the hills, for we owe it everything.

20th January - 1962

All Set for the Supper

By this time the Burns Supperers will have all their arrangements made for the feast which is the last and finest in Scotland's January canon. The scene is set, the pipe and tabor arranged, and the celebrant of the Immortal Memory all booked up.

Nothing remains save to hope madly that the snow keeps off long enough for congregation, acolyte, and celebrant to arrive dead on time. The faithful cannot help wishing that the poet had chosen his birthday with more regard for co-operative weather. So does the principal speaker who suddenly finds himself clutching the notes for his remarks with one hand as he slews his Land-Rover "past the birks and Meikle stane" right into the frustrating depths of a snowdrift with the other.

Luckily at this season there is always some helpful inhabitant at hand to offer his services and those of his tractor with decent civility. But it all takes time, and while the traveller waits he wonders just how late he is going to be. But there is comfort in reflecting that there is inevitably a toast list of formidable length before his turn comes us. There is the "Queen, God Bless Her."

It is a pity the blessings are of short duration in terms of public speaking. The "Armed Forces," though, ought to make up. Twenty minutes at least in an impeccable English accent. Good show!

Probably the "Ladies" will come along then or are they after "Agriculture and the Plough"? Anyway sometimes it is a good thing to escape the "Ladies," especially when the audience is mixed. Wives and sweethearts have a way of not being so broadminded as one could expect in these modern days. Their chilly unamused glance can kill the bravura stone dead.

And on the subject of wives, has his own wife seen to it that his digestive tablets are in this jacket pocket? Haggis never did sit comfortably on his tummy. Too much spice and stuff that looks like minced leather with a strong smell of sheep. Nor do the accompaniments help; the turnip is never mashed smoothly enough, neither are the potatoes and both vegetables barely escape being cold.

Naturally much depends on the venue. In a reasonable hotel all will be piping hot – in every sense. The rurals and other women's organisations who go for the poet in a big way serve complicated meals at the maximum inconvenience to themselves and the minimum enjoyment of their guests.

* * *

Agitated by delay, already suffering prophetic pangs of indigestion, the speaker finally boards his car to make his slippery way to journey's end where he finds a flurry of anxious tartan eddying from look-out post to banquet hall.

All now seems well and when he glances down the programme he finds he has escaped the haggis (piping, address, and consumption), but has not escaped Tam o' Shanter recited by a fiery particle of a man who has learned the poem by heart while in hospital with a broken leg and time on his hands.

Declaimed at two hundred words per second, the poem comes over with the inevitability of genius. But the speaker, cutting course and drinks to equalise timing, is not there to . . . literary criticism . . . for his supper . . . Not but what . . . Scottish lives . . .

(Sadly the rest of this article has been lost - editor)

Europe Seen from a Small Farm

January is as nearly over as makes no difference and still the weather continues abominable, with the wind and snow whooping it up out of Siberia with most uncomradely malice.

The Laich farmers are as "sair made" as we are up in the hills for they are sadly behind with their spring cultivations. For both of us, hillman and plainsman, the angry winter day passes in attending to our beasts and thinking troubled thoughts about how new policies and trends must influence the way we make our living. Mr Jenkins and the Common Market between them have stolen the agricultural headlines and it is inevitable that both should dominate any farming conversation.

* * *

Most of us in the North-East belong to that category of "small farm" which Mr Jenkins would like to scrutinise carefully. The N.F.U. raised a furious racket about his comments but I doubt if the individual farmers here are all that angry.

In the first place none of us really believes he is all that small, and in the second we take the union's championship with a grain of cynical salt. We are fully aware that we have been stung for a higher subscription and the officials must show willing if they are not to lose our membership. While admitting that the union has its uses on a national level many of us remain unimpressed by its handling of our local difficulties. If Mr Jenkins has stirred up our branches to consider their members' immediate interests we are all for Mr Jenkins. Up the rebels!

But the Common Market is another pair of shoes. In spite of all the soothing syrup administered by Messrs Butler and Maclay we are all sure hereabouts that we are for the high jump into Europe. Nor are we as scared as might seem. After all anyone who has been farming all his life in the hazards of a Scottish climate can never acknowledge dismay.

It is true that we look askance at a completely new system of payment. Understandably we are reluctant to exchange the known for the unknown even though we are lamentably aware of the snags in the known. Every one knows we have been sanctimonious at the top of our voices about the subsidy payment on beef cattle. Nor are other subsidy payments entirely free from muddle.

Why a claim for hill drains can be scrutinised and paid for inside a week but payment for a calf subsidy needs three months to come up is more than some of us can understand.

Since all these matters affect us so intimately we may be forgiven for thinking thus egotistically. But eventually even farmers come to, and realize that others are involved with them.

The Road to Spring in Sight Once More

Just as January makes its first tentative steps across February's threshold, the moor road emerges from the murk in which it has lain since November; and the sight of its shabby verges rejoices me more than any vista beckoning with a rainbow.

For the emergent road is a sure sign that spring is on the way back; Persephone is returning from the halls of Dis to the upper air.

The road that tells me all this is little better than a path, winding past ruined crofts, through moor grass, and over broken bogs to find its undistinguished conclusion in hill farms in Dallas. No one uses it save the gamekeeper and the shepherd, for its dreich environs offer no inducement to the adventurous. Yet looking north from our windows, its outline is sharp and definite against the rolling hill.

Some trick of light renders it invisible during the winter months but come spring the road is at once a landmark. Perhaps it does not fire the imagination, but since it is an integral part of our landscape it has its own value for us.

Countrymen living among scenes of natural magnificence are not in the habit of viewing them with the informed eye of the artist or even of the appreciative visitor. Morven rising blue and symmetrical out of the wine dark sea; Darnaway with its forest etched against skies red from the cautery of frost, do not move us because they are lovely. We accept them as parts of ourselves. They are our hands, our feet, our hearts.

They have the dear familiarity of blood, and only when we are divorced from them do we become aware of our patrimony.

Mountains, burns, and even my dubby little road are suddenly realized to have qualities more human than scenic. We miss them as friends, and long for them as members of our family.

For strangers settling here, the matter may turn out quite differently. Not everyone enjoys the proximity of mountains and to have the hills looking at you through the window may well be disconcerting.

If you come from the plain you may long for the uncluttered horizons of your own land, while the river roaring its head off above the ice floes of obstinate winter may not be as reassuring as a chat with the woman next door. Then solitude becomes another name for loneliness and the moor birds call not a song, but the cry of a breaking heart.

But for those born into the country, home is where the mountains rise and rivers run. Not far from here over the moor lived an old lady on a farm which is now only a grazing. No road led to her door though the railway passes quite near. She knew no modern convenience. Her little cottage stood on a green knoll with a clump of indigenous pines to shelter it from the wind.

Some years ago a kindly laird engineered her removal to a place much more convenient. The old lady was delighted for 10 days and then she pined. The laird, who was understanding, as well as kind, had her taken back with all her gear. Her household goods, never having left the place, awaited her. And so she lived happily ever after. The elements were her children and the moor her ancestor.

How Not to Buy a Bull

October and February are red-letter months in the cattle farmer's calendar. In October he sells his season's crop of calves, and in February he decides on the kind of bull he wishes to use in his herd.

Since bulls are inescapable facts of life on a stock farm, everyone interested acts with as much foresight and energy as possible. Local papers are clamorous with advertisements for forthcoming bull sales, and intending buyers mark such dates with a cross.

Of course, the bull sale with real cachet is Perth, where already the Aberdeen-Angus sales are over. Perth is famous for fair maids, Pullars, and cattle; and the last named is the most famous. Every stock farmer who can makes for Perth in February. Not all go to buy, and still fewer go to sell, but all want to be present at an event as exotic as expensive, as international as dramatic.

Once the great sales are over, their consequences reverberate wherever cattle policies are made. This year, when price reviewers and statutory boarders are joining the ranks of Tuscany, Perth, 1962, may well take a memorable place in agricultural history.

Farmers who go to these sales as spectators come home to buy their bulls at the mart where they are acquainted with the auctioneer and the judges. The set-up they find less daunting than in Perth, and on the home stamping ground you do not have to work out sums in Argentine currency nor buy an expensive catalogue to enter to the sale ring.

* * *

The bulls for sale do not have the plushy grooming of their more aristocratic brothers, but neither do they look like overstuffed furniture moving around on castors instead of legs. What the ordinary man wants is a beast who will give him calves with a bit of size about them as well as the ability to carry flesh. Many notable breeders who care about the home market put forward consignments of just such beasts, and if the prices paid are not so fancy as at Perth they are profitable enough.

But the earnest small farmer who is in search of a bull need not even go to his local mart to find one. He may instead employ the secret agent routine. This means that he drops casually in at a friend's farm and after craftily leading the conversation round to cattle he goes off to study his pal's stock. The two men spend a pleasant hour brooding over the beasts and, having analysed the calves from lug to hair, from haunch to nose, the prospective buyer departs in a haze.

Negotiations are resumed some days later, for after all one cannot procrastinate indefinitely when it is a question of the date of next year's calf crop. Eventually the deal is completed and the new owner keeps his fingers crossed hoping the bull will leave only stot calves.

No one has ever done what I once did. I bought a bull over the telephone without seeing him. His owner was an old friend and he assured me that the bull was a jewel. When he came home I was terrified for he was yelling blue murder all over the glen. It took an old angry Irish cow called Biddy to calm him down sufficiently for me to look him over. He was hideous. Strangely his calves were all I could wish for. But I shouldn't buy a bull that way again.

17th February - 1962

A New Minister
is Inducted

After six months' uneasy interregnum between one minister going and another coming to take his place the congregation in this scattered upland parish gathered for the induction in which they welcomed their new pastor and heard him take the solemn vows which bind him to kirk and parishioner. As inductions here seem to occur but once in the quarter of a century the event was one of singularity as well as significance.

The appointed night was bitter. "The owl for all his feathers was a-cold," and well he might be, for the earth rang beneath the hammer blows of frost which sent the stars streaming off into a shower of sparks to blaze above our little kirk, standing foursquare and Presbyterian in the neuk of the river which has been her stance since before the '15.

Parishioners and friends, ministers and presbyters, came from all the airts, so that the small interior was packed with folk; every Scots face more Scots than usual. It was one of those rare moments which discover us to ourselves – a people intense but dour, idiosyncratic but orthodox.

Our pipe organ – a gift from one of the line of generous lairds we enjoy – pealed and then the ministers took over. They filed in, rustling in stiff Geneva silks, the hoods of their Scottish universities, as sombre as splendid, hanging from their shoulders to contrast with the snowdrop whiteness of their bands.

* * *

The Reformation is still a vivid memory with us and these men are its immediate heirs. True the purple velvet blowing in a draught on the lectern and the brass bowl of hyacinths on the communion table would have been anathema to the Calvinists, but the faces of the men who wear gown and bands have the same expressions of turbulent spirituality contained by theology which must have been worn by their predecessors more than 400 years ago. Full of logical high purpose the stern Presbyterian ceremony took its way.

Then in the middle of a prayer the electric light went out without even a warning flicker; but such was the solemnity of the occasion and the placid faith of the man who prayed that not a sigh went up from the worshippers. The service proceeded with torches gravely handed up to the pulpit that the Bible might be the more conveniently read.

A few small lights broke out desultorily to show latecomers delayed by snow-bound roads to their places. In the eerie flicker a brass memorial tablet gleamed for a moment to remind us of the soldiers, scholars, divines, and viceroys who had prayed here before going from this desolate corner of a winter moor to find renown in a wide world.

Still without lights, the congregation rose to sing the 23rd Psalm. With no organ, no choir, only grave puritan fervour rescued us from the awkward moment. "Yea though I walk through death's dark vale," we sang; and the lights came on once more.

Individual Treatment for Contented Cows

Though there is only a bare half week in February left, we still are scared to believe that spring's intentions are honourable. Who could blame us for doubting?

We have had one of the longest and stormiest of winters. Snowfalls alternated with half-hearted thaws till we longed with all our hearts for a spell of good clean frost. But to-day larks are singing and thrushes brush up their arpeggios in the beeches. The sky gives a pale repentant smile and the last rotten wreath in the back road disintegrates.

Perhaps by to-morrow the access path will look like itself and not twin to the bed of a burn in spate. I don't know how long it will take the fields to lose their appearance of having been washed up out of the ocean or the poor drowned grass to cease resembling seaweed.

A winter like this is hard on beast and man. Here, where a fair part of farm income is derived from wintering sheep, we are naturally anxious to do our best for our woolly boarders. In a normal season we expect to get them acclimatised to the hill, so that by the end of December they are in good fettle for the bad weather of January.

This winter the first snow came in the middle of November, so that we had to have recourse to hand feeding six weeks earlier than usual. We fed hay, but some of our neighbours turned their flocks into a portion of the turnip ground. With their nimble hooves dancing to their own version of a well known broadcasting dancing teacher's theme, they quickly beat out the tune of "Snow, snow, thaw, thaw, snow" above the neeps, with the catastrophic effect of burying them under a thick layer of impacted ice.

We could have tholed the storms and their bitter inconvenience if only we had not had mud to contend with as well. Our two silage pits where the cattle self-feed have been quite something. Old Morag from Skye said that if Dod expected her to go and take her breakfast with her feet up to the knees in sludge he had another think coming. She'd rather starve, so she would.

If she had to eat silage he could bring it to her. And the poor mutt did. Over it, served comfortably in her stall, she indicated that a bit of nice short sheep hay would give it a relish. If that was a pail of draff in the corner she did not fancy it so much as a pan full of cake. So she has passed the most comfortable winter of the lot of us.

Eventually some of the other cows tumbled to it that she was on to a good thing and began to think up plans to allow them to follow her example. Maudie coyly promised she'd rear two calves if she got V.I.P. treatment. So Dod took her in. Then Greta fussed so much about her son Julius not being able to stand up to the spartan conditions, that he was housed – and as mother was his meal ticket, Greta took up a stall next to Maudie.

Finally there is N'old. Dod bought N'old a week from calving in Inverness. She is a kind-hearted old thing and used to bracing treatment – or so it would appear. She went off quietly to the cold hillside to produce her little bull calf. She demanded nothing and was so generally uncomplaining and brave that Dod took her home, and she also got a place in the byre. She is so grateful for the smallest extra we feel quite ashamed for the greed and selfishness of the rest of the herd.

Comforting isn't it, that sometimes virtue is rewarded?

Culture and a Country Cousin

One of the things I miss most when imprisoned on the snow-bound moor of upland winter is the weekly visit to Elgin and my jaunt to the library. Elgin is extremely lucky in the site of its library, for it uses an old mansion house to keep its books.

The elegant place, all windows and the odd powder closet, stands in the middle of a park where the ruined cathedral emanates serenity on one hand; while swans compose an eternal ballet by a willowed island on the other.

For two pins you'd swear you caught a glimpse of Florentius Volusenus in his monkish habit strolling home to add a chapter to his "De Animi Tranquillitate," or read the latest letter from Du Bellay out of France.

For many years our library, immersed in the sedative ecclesiastical influences proper to its environment, pursued its antique way. Its patrons, once over the worn sandstone step, found themselves in a hall full of what looked like wooden nest boxes from a deep litter shed. These were the containers for the books which were due to go to the little county libraries housed in the schools.

The library proper was in two parts. The town portion was upstairs, which perhaps accounted for its slightly guilty air of having been sent to the attic.

The county library was packed into one magnificent room where the librarian grew cacti in the window over the radiator while she attended to the books and us. The rest of the building was taken up with an incongruous tearoom and a reading room more notable for its views than its periodicals.

* * *

The one room county library was where everyone congregated. It was the sunniest, most glorious hugger-mugger imaginable. When you wanted a book you just howked and if you did not find it the librarian did – just like that. "From the Gracchi to Nero" or "Doctor Zhivago," she knew where to lay her hand on either.

Because of the overcrowding only one reader at a time could insinuate himself between the aisles of book cases; but one could always lend a helping eye if someone, who had missed his place in the queue for the *cul de sac*, was in a hurry.

When we wanted new books we subscribed so much per year and told our dear little librarian what we wanted and she got it. As we were all highly peculiar people with definite tastes the result was not only interesting but lurid. We read each other's books, commenting irascibly the while. We took our dogs into the library where they behaved impeccably because the librarian fed them chocolate biscuits; in return we gave her such unlikely gifts as a few fresh eggs or a box of camellias.

Then the halcyon days ended. The city fathers were alerted to the fact that this was no way to disseminate sweetness and light in an up-and-coming town like Elgin. More people than weirdies who took their fiction hot and their erudition neat must be catered for. So the experts came in and found dry rot and other things, not com-gracious living. Once . . . had finished. The . . . came along to . . . cracked ceilings . . .

(Sadly the rest of this article has been lost - editor)

Beautiful, Though Comfortless

Daffodils may come before the swallow dares, but that's along the Bohemian shore and not on the outskirts of Dava Moor, where their golden trumpets and gallant spears lie buried at this precise moment in deep snow.

Last week-end brought the blizzard that was father and mother to all the other blizzards of this weary winter. The result is that this morning every moorland farm lies quilted to the eaves in the heavy glistering blanket which has turned us into the prettiest, most unseasonable picture imaginable.

Since there was no wind, but just a steady, eident three days' fall, two level feet of snow lie over all. Roofs, fences, trees, all bear the same weight; but as some are more fitted to sustain it than others, odd accidents occur. Garage roofs seem to have been the greatest sufferers and our local garage terrified its proprieter out of his wits when, with a loud premonitory crack of its timbers, it signified its instant intention of caving in. Hastily seizing the bare essentials of his trade the owner fled the scene and now pursues his calling alfresco, in a temperature too cold to be bracing.

Fences, on the other hand, appreciate the chance to wear diamond tiaras which look very effective against the strong blue of the sky and the bright sun. They gain much by being geometrically laid out and span their brave rectangular constellation over the flanks of moor and hill.

* * *

43

The trees present nothing like so spectacular an appearance. The small ones in the up and coming plantations use their young resilience to bow beneath their burden; but if they are mature, they fare less safely since their great limbs crack and splinter under the dead, intolerable weight.

Because it is March, the sun shines longer, and this lures the birds up from the Laich. Yesterday, a flurry of lapwings appeared. One wonders why they came, for the twenty-third of the month is the date they are in the habit of choosing for their spring flitting.

Perhaps some quality in the light is responsible for tempting such birds inland. After all, we use artificial light to stimulate the pituitary gland in domestic fowls kept in deep litter, to deceive them into thinking spring has come, so probably a similar mechanism is operative among wild birds. However the party preferred to keep their glands in status quo for they beat a hasty retreat, melodiously jeered on their way by the chaffinches who were eating greedily at our neighbour's bird table and looking dead natty in braw new rose-coloured waistcoats.

* * *

There seems no prospect for a swift thaw for all the sun shines so encouragingly. For real business we require a warm wind, and so far the winds are still coming to us from the fields of snow. I hope we do not have to go on being beautiful but comfortless indefinitely. The tasks of spring are piling up alarmingly.

We do not yearn to plough our stony inhospitable acres even for a plough-up subsidy, but we do want to get fertiliser on the grass. Dod bought a wonderful new bone davey warranted to spread fertiliser with clockwork precision. At the price it ought to provide the fertiliser as well. Still, it would be pleasant to use it.

Looking after the beasts keeps us from too many reflections, and for once the silage pits look like making the new grass without any undue skimping. This ought to save us having to run about the country carting all the bits and pieces an empty larder makes you go out and find. And come a week of warm sun and black ground we'll be so restored in hope and spirit as we'd not call the King our cousin.

The Share System

When, after the cumulating storms of the past winter, we found the entrances to both silage pits full to the neck with not only the usual slushy slurry but avalanches as well, we rang a neighbour who does the odd spot of contracting and asked him if he could come with his bulldozing tackle and cope. So he came – and coped.

He worked for a whole day and half an hour. The whole day was for excavating the pits; the half-hour for digging out a path to the garage where our car had been lying in the deep freeze for 10 days. We were all delighted; our friend because he thus recovered something of the heavy capital cost of his equipment; ourselves because we did not have to buy the implements for this occasional but essential use.

A common way of acquiring expensive farm machinery in these parts is to buy the tool and then have it work its passage by contracting with it. The district has set itself up in corn drills and crop sprayers by this means and now is working its way up into the combine harvester, hay baler status. While the method may be convenient for the individual farmer, I doubt whether it makes sense in the wider context, for it seems mad that every minus-a-100-acre holding should possess the rafts of implements you see lying round the place. Surely a full-time contracting service might be the answer.

There are two things against this. First, there is the now deeply engrained habit of buying a tool on the self help system. Because the farmer who owns the fancy toy knows that the only way to keep it in decent repair is to operate it himself, he turns up in person on your place to do what is required. Naturally you get a good job, but the farmer-contractor ignores the massive fact in agricultural finance which is that you do not have to pay yourself overtime. Therefore he renders you a bill far less than a real contractor would.

Obviously no contractor then can compete for our custom. It is just too bad, that once the implement has earned its buying price the farmer ceases to contract with it. Which is where we came in.

Secondly, there is the weather. The truth is that if you insist on farming in a capricious climate you must have what you want when you want it. There is no use hanging about in spring waiting for the corn drill when waiting as like as not means that you are to suffer from the teuchat storm, the lambing storm, the gab of May, or any other of the woeful tempests of the far from merry Scottish spring. If you except a harvest you must get the seed in at the proper time, and never mind the soothing myths that say when the birk buds are the size of a mouse's ear is time enough.

Similarly at hay or harvest time you dare not delay, for speed is once more of the essence. So you had better work out – and quick-whether 'tis nobler in the mind to suffer the wastage of a whole hay crop or to take arms against your bank manager and buy a hay baler – or combine harvester.

During the Second World War the A.E.C.s ran a contracting service for farmers. In those days we could not buy machinery if we would, and the service ran wonderfully well considering. But the minute controls came off we queued up to blow our profits in expensive outfits which soon became out of date. The "goavermint," as we called the contracting service, had been looking askance for some time at its mounting deficit, and, seeing our reaction, delightedly packed up and left us to it.

The Last Lap of Wintering

A friend has just been in to make a phone call to the remoter regions of the west where the owner of the sheep he is wintering lives. Telephones in the country seem to be suffering from the general malaise due to climatic conditions which afflict the rest of us, for when we tried to make the call they either bared their fangs in a black vulcanite snarl, or relapsed into remote silence punctuated by orbital clicks.

So in the end the arrangements about the inoculations for the sheep against tick ere they return to their native heaths, remained in the limbo of the great unspoken. Which will turn out to be a great nuisance since this inoculation has to be done a fortnight before it is effective and there remains but a bare week before the flock return at the end of the wintering season. We are sorry about the non-inoculation, but elated at the idea of the last lap of the wintering.

This has been one of the most expensive winters we have known in upland Moray. Most of us began hand feeding back in January and have continued it ever since. Because of the unrelenting depth of snow, turnips, which are the usual feed in such circumstances, were unobtainable and we were forced into feeding hay; hay which at upwards of £16 a ton gives a top-heavy look to our merchant's bills.

We ourselves are feeding four hundredweights of hay a day. Teased out of its bale and twine it looks an awful mountain of stuff, but the sheep make short work of it. Dod stuffs it into makeshift troughs of netting wire strung along a fence and you should see the way the sheep attack it. They hurl themselves down a small slope, kicking, pushing, and shoving one another and they devour the fodder voraciously, acting more like wolves than sheep. Once they devour their food they retire a small way off and chew their ravening cuds till it is time for the next meal. The snow is too deep for them to forage widely so they have become conditioned to remaining in one place and waiting for attention.

* * *

We wonder whether their owner will be pleased at the reappearance on his place of nearly 300 hogs with an imperious look in their eye and the habit of being waited on.

In normal years, the moss crop is widespread on the hill at this time. (I am not sure what name other people give to this herbage, which is really the early stage of cotton grass.) But anyway, it appears to have wonderful feeding properties and sheep and cattle eating it with avidity seem to grow visibly as they feed. This season it is buried under snow where we presume it leads the subterranean life of a deep freeze troglodyte.

There is this to be said for sheep who cannot wander the wide hill – they stay put and your count is a lot less likely to be short. In a way we hope the weather conditions continue thus for we have no mind to have sheep going off to commit suicide in slushy burns and bogs.

Guest Speakers

Now that summertime is officially upon us, albeit with more regard for bureaucratic convenience than seasonal accuracy, secretaries of local activities thankfully announce their final meeting of the session.

They then stagger off to put themselves out to grass till July, when they must get back into orbit, uttering as they "orb" their sad, familiar cry: - "It's so difficult to get speakers."

The other day we were all shaken to the core by a report in a northern newspaper of a Sassenach who expressed surprise at the way we treat the speaker in Scotland. He said that in other countries (England and all) they not only pay their speakers but take it for granted that they should do so.

In Scotland, on the other hand, we treat the speaker as our ancestors treated the wandering minstrel; we give him his supper and a warm place by the fire.

As an itinerant speaker, it would ill become me to go all the way with the surprised Englishman; for I have usually been treated with great kindness and courtesy; though if pushed by extreme cross-examination I should have to admit that I have rarely been offered a fee. After the party everyone clusters round with many complimentary words, which may sometimes fall on stony ground.

On one of these occasions a beaming matron, fair taken on with herself and her own graciousness, bore down on me explaining as she sailed that actually she'd have preferred to have gone to another rammy where they were running a course in flower arrangement, but she felt it her duty to come to the present affair as she was an office-bearer.

Most local activities here are run by women, and it says much for their organising abilities that the kirk guilds, rurals, and their urban sister townswomen's guilds flourish in spite of difficulties, both monetary and temperamental. They work out an equilibrium of experience which keeps them going; and the stresses to which they may become liable are so well understood that built-in equalisers automatically take over when something looks like coming apart.

In this they are much more fortunate than dramatic societies. If there is one parish activity more than another warranted to set the glen in a lowe it is the Dramatic. Perhaps it feels it has a name to live up to; but from the word "Go," when the play to be produced is being chosen, the Dramatic lurches from emotional crisis to emotional crisis.

* * *

Some members may become so incensed that they hive off in mid-air to become another body, for the "splitted splits" are a favourite metaphysical recreation of the Scots. At other times a vindictive clique may kid the parent body along with the excuse that though they have not attended rehearsals with the regularity expected, it will be "all right on the night." Then when everything is set, down to future engagements, the clique can declare they are opting out.

There is no end to the fiendish ingenuities which can burst the Dramatic wide open. When a play does reach the boards of the village hall I am uncertain whether to receive it in the spirit of the drama or regard it as another battle honour for the producer.

Cat and Bull Story

For many years a small tortoiseshell cat called Pansy lived with us. She possessed an intelligence as formidable as her character, so that she regarded us with that affectionate contempt one uses towards an uncomplaining convenience.

This meant that when she was inadvertently caught in a rabbit snare she realised the futility of struggling and so hanging herself. A human, she knew, would soon come along to free her, so she settled down to await the event. Sure enough the human did come and she was released. Her behaviour was most gracious and by the time she had finished purring and stroking her rescuer he felt he had just been awarded the George Cross.

But although she trusted us so far, there were limits to her confidence and these limits warned her that it would be unsafe to regard kittens as falling within their bounds. Kittens she must look out for by herself. She devised the most devilishly hidden nurseries for them until she hit on one that was quite human proof. This was in a corner of the bull's pen.

At that time I owned an Ayrshire bull which I had brought up from the calf stage. All Ayrshire bulls are temperamental and Frankie was no exception. It was true he had a moderately soft spot for me but for no one else.

* * *

But even I did not care to presume upon an old affection, so Pansy's family were safe as long as they remained with Frankie. I did think she was not as grateful as she might have been for his affording her sanctuary since she would swear green glittering murder if he looked like putting a snort or a horn wrong.

All during the kitten-rearing stage she came back and forth to the scullery for her food, and then took a little time off to put her poor feet up on the old sofa, purring with pleasure at our company. When she was not bowed down with family cares she lived almost completely in the house, kindly accepting our hospitality until, one day, Smiler arrived. No one knew Smiler's origins, but she was an insinuating little creature with impeccable social habits, so that before we knew it Smiler was established by the fender.

Pansy was livid, swearing beneath her breath when we were present and scratching Smiler when we were absent. Smiler just smiled – whereupon Pansy swept grandly out and went off to live with our neighbours, who are rather suckers about cats.

Pansy made a great fuss of them and arranged that we should see her giving a wonderful impersonation of the faithful animal who lived only for her masters. She was quite disgusting, sitting patiently at their door yearning to acknowledge their care for the unloved waif.

She kept up this horrid fulsomeness for a year and at the end of that time she had us so ashamed that we were afraid to look in her amber eye and read her condemnation of our inconstancy.

Last week-end our neighbours said they were going off for a short holiday and they indicated Pansy sitting on a window-sill cutting us dead. Would we, they wondered, feed Pansy?

We said we would do what we could to help, but we were doubtful about the outcome. Pansy washed her face and dismissed us from the audience. That was on the Friday. On the Sunday she knocked imperiously at the window. "What's for supper?" she asked with the effrontery which always pays off. I meekly fed her. She ate vastly and then, as of yore, retired to the sofa.

Smiler, who had been out, then came home. "Still got THAT CAT," remarked Pansy. Smiler replied with a vulgar spit. So now I arrange that Smiler uses the sitting-room while Pansy monopolises the kitchen. When our neighbours return I expect another arrangement will be made by Pansy.

Perks for Farmers' Wives

I read with avid interest a furious letter in a farming paper written by a farmer about hens, money, and farmers' wives. The gist of the matter is that 75 per cent of the present production of eggs in this country comes from the small producer who does not know whether hens pay or not.

The bulk of these small producers are farmers' wives who do not care a docken whether eggs are half a crown or three shillings because they keep their hens "on the strength," wangling the layers' pellets on to the general feeding stuffs bill and pinching corn out of the loft to conceal it from their husbands' views.

* * *

Thus with feminine guile they get themselves out from under the feed bill and as a result the egg money wears the delightful air of something for nothing. The writer went on to say that he did not blame Eve for this sleight of hand because he knew that only by exercising it could she get a housekeeping allowance plus a bob to spend on herself.

That the egg money should keep the house going is one of the oldest farming traditions and every farmer's wife – except me – is happy with the arrangement. How generously it works out in practice varies with the farm and the husband. One wife may get all the egg money to use as she sees fit, though even this lavish attitude presupposes that she buys her own replacements out of income.

And, of course, she does the actual poultry-keeping which is no small labour.

* * *

In another case the henwife may be expected to do much more with the egg money. One of my own old friends ran the house, clothed herself and the children, paid incidental schooling accounts, and financed running household repairs all out of the egg money. She continued to do this till the children reached university stage when she announced firmly that the farm must take on the further education bills.

Until fairly recently pigs were also a source of pin money for the farm wife. Before we had discovered the convenience of the Milk Marketeers who now dump pints of milk at every farm road end we had to have a dairy cow to provide our own supply. In the summer in the flush of grass the cow gave a flush of milk. A useful way of dealing with this surplus was to keep a pig (or maybe two) and feed it with a mixture of milk and household scraps together with odds and ends of barley.

The great advantage for some women was that when they sold the pigs they got a lump sum of money all at once. Eggs, on the other hand, were paid for every week, which was certainly convenient for dealing with the house-keeping bill, though one never had the delicious illusion of being rich which came from the pig sale. It all depended on your psyche which method you favoured.

But the piggy as a perk has become obsolete owing to the exasperating Danes who, by force of good example, have forced pig farming into big and therefore efficient business. The carefree days of cheerful slapdashery in feeding pigs are gone for ever. I wonder how long it will be before eggs follow bacon. Even the most conservative farming household cannot continue indefinitely oblivious about costs, especially as the advantages of the huge professional poultry units become daily more striking. They can buy in bulk, economise in labour, and have the edge in transport costs since it is clearly cheaper to collect a hundred cases at once than go haring all over the place picking up the odd few dozen.

The farmer letter-writer suggests that hens and eggs should be abandoned as the wife's perks and her husband should pay her a wage instead. Hasten the day.

Winter Sports Bring New Life

In Easter week-end the landscape still wears its snowy aspect. True, the lapwings swoop in the thin wind but their acrobatics lack true spring ardour, while the grouse, dispirited by the atmosphere that sweeps from mountains as corniced high in snow as their corries are deep in the stuff, utter the odd disillusioned cackle that romance is old hat.

The only creatures invigorated by continuing winter are the skiers who, judging by the speed with which they flash by our road-end, just cannot wait to make the Cairngorms. By the appearance of things, winter sports look like carrying on into May and maybe – Scotland's summer being what it is – extending all the year round.

* * *

Those of us whose interests and life's work lie elsewhere are hanging about waiting for the fertilisers to come in, so we have a moment to look around us. Absorbing to the exclusion of much else as farming in the foothills of a mountainous region must be, even we – preoccupied with beasts and new grants for winter keep and the mysteries of the Common Market – cannot be impervious to the change that is taking place, if not in our immediate neighbourhood, at least in the vicinity.

We cannot turn our beasts from one field to another across the road without being aware of the stream of cars all zooming up to Grantown with skis lashed securely to their roofs. Not so long ago such winter traffic was a ferly and we could count on getting our herd moved at their own pace over the highway. Now we begin to think we shall have to put a large admonitory notice saying "Caution, Cows Crossing!"

Nor is the odd farmer the only person who feels the repercussions. The small local papers are full of complaints about the economy of the district being increasingly geared to the ski-tourist industry. The new ski road is kept open when the indigenous inhabitants have to plowter about as they can on their own snow drifted communications. So the Letters to Editor allege.

Even counties take up cudgels against one another and Inverness-shire thinks not without reason that Moray since it embraces Grantown – one of the big skiing resorts – should help to foot the bill for maintaining and clearance. Dark words about making the ski road subject to tolls are ceasing to be muttered only in corners but are being increasingly heard in pubs and written in newssheets.

That such a vigorous expanding industry should make this impact on what was recently a Highland backwater is not surprising. Of course some people groan and entrenched conservatives tune up their pibrochs. But now that bets are beginning to be laid in pubs on the outcome of the next slalom and schoolchildren talk knowledgeably about Swiss styles and Norwegian styles in skiing, the last atavistic citadels would seem to be conquered.

There is something exciting in watching new life fountaining back into a dying countryside. Two years ago I visited a small Highland hotel in the area. It had been taken over by new owners who were busy lifting the linoleum from the stair treads and removing the stuffed trout from the parlour. Last year I returned to superb cooking, superb beds, and heavenly central heating.

This year there are two skiing schools in the village and my hotel is doing a roaring trade in packed lunches and the hiring of ski-equipment. The accents of Swiss French crackle in the crisp air along with Austrian dialects, while native Gaels enchanted at not having to be melancholy any more allow their own ebullience to welcome the stranger with grace and imagination.

Where My Caravan is Resting

The welter of holiday traffic starts earlier every year so that, though it is not May yet, the surge on our moor road thickens daily. There are many caravans in the tide and you should hear the exasperated screams of commercial lorries on our few straight stretches trying to pass these yawing vehicles before the next dizzy corner. No wonder caravanners keep a well-thumbed list of authorized caravan sites along with the map in the front pocket.

Sites for caravans are becoming big business in a countryside which is sensible enough to cash in on its tourist attractions; and farmers who not so long ago regarded the holidaymaker as an intruder now see that catering for him will make a useful alternative to the traditional sidelines of pig and poultry keeping, which are not nearly so lucrative as they were. To go over from deep-litter hens to caravan siting is, however, considerably more difficult than to switch from pig-keeping to calf-rearing, for, though the caravanner may have a romantic notion for a spot of rugged adventure, the county authorities have no intention of letting him set up holiday quarters in a disintegrating farm square or by the abandoned nest boxes of the big litter shed. He must be looked after whether he wants it or not.

* * *

Before setting up a caravan site plans have to be submitted to the planning people and an opportunity given for objectors to blow their tops. After the hysterics have died down the public health authorities then move in and demand that plans for the proper provision of water stands, lavatory accommodation, bathrooms, wash-up places, refuse disposal, and what have you, be forthcoming for their approval. Anyone who has seen the horrid chaos that can prevail on a non-authorised site knows too well that such precautions are necessary.

And it has to be remembered that many caravan stances cater for the permanent van dweller as well as his holidaying brother. Pirate sites do spring up overnight, but they do not last more than a few weeks, for the sanitary people attack them with statute and disinfectant and drum them out of existence.

Thus one might imagine that the lot of the caravanner, permanent or passing, is completely untroubled, confidently sunny. And so it would be if it were not for the little matter of housekeeping supplies. Many of the sites are on privately owned farmland, and the farmer has no intention of allowing any Tom, Dick, or Harry of a mobile shop free access to a tidy ready-made market. Which is fair enough.

Further, the farmer himself has found that it is a very short step to take from selling farm produce to setting up a general merchant's place of his own. Sensibly he realises that there are some products he cannot easily handle; bread is one of them and butcher-meat another. So what he does is to arrange with a baker and a butcher to come along and pay him for the privilege of selling to the caravanners. Thus it all adds up to a cute little monopoly – completely legal but nonetheless infuriating.

For the holidaymaker the convenience of having a shop on the doorstep will outweigh the compulsion, but the permanent van-holder may have different feelings. Even a simple mind can figure out the inconvenient consequences that may follow from a resolute refusal to deal with the landlord's store.

A Place for a Happy Holiday

In the state of advanced morbidity from which report alleges all Scottish industry suffers it is comforting to find a potential money spinner in the back garden – and I don't mean farming.

Here in the North-East we are sitting on the fringe of one of the finest natural playgrounds in Britain, and it is difficult to remain for ever in the doldrums when so many entertaining pursuits coax you to come outside and play. You can ride, walk, or climb; you can winter sport or golf, you can swim and yacht. Are you still not interested? Then what about fishing and shooting? Well, do you fancy archery?

If you must still be choosey I've no doubt that by this time some enterprising bloke in the Findhorn valley has learned that falconry used to be a fashionable pursuit here in 1290 and is even now getting ready to teach you the elements of the charming and ancient art. You'd certainly be eye-catching if you went to the office with a peregrine complete with hood, bells, and jesses on your wrist.

* * *

But perhaps you are the introverted type? Then we can do you a line in glamour and romance, though it is but fair to warn you that damp, draughts, and midges are often to be encountered in Highland castles and majestic scenery. Give us a year or two, though, and we'll have our ruins and our legends slicked up to match our hotels, on which we have done quite a smooth job.

No one seems to have noticed the miraculous and happy change effected in the Highland hotel since the Hydro boys made the immersion heater a commonplace and a family firm in Fochabers upped and canned the exquisite foods of the countryside to export all over the world.

Last year Morayshire gave the Queen and Prince Philip a smashing lunch from local products. There was Spey salmon and new picked raspberries and cream. The cream was real cow cream and was served in great glass jugs with the faintest flowering of frost on the outside to give proper emphasis to the suave golden fragrance of the cream inside. And the county can do the same for you any summer day you care – forbye serving it at the hands of waiters wearing tartan jackets to match the stair carpet on the hotel stairs.

* * *

We have come along way but we are not complacent even if we have a ski road and a lift. We'd like to give a new look to two of our oldest sports, fishing and shooting. Fishing is in danger of becoming too rarefied for the novice who gets bored by academic jargon on whether a grouse and claret is better than a cockybondoo in a balanced cast for broken water. What he wants to experience is the gasping excitement of fishing the midnight rise when the fool trout will snap any lure, or the intoxication of trolling from a boat for the noble ferox trout.

Grouse shooting is suffering from disease and the "toffs." The former has caused the death of great numbers of the only species of bird exclusively British; the latter have emphasised the exclusiveness of the sport, as if only they were capable of enjoying the guns, gillies, and gorgeous tweeds that are the accompaniments of a day spent under the blue sky on a honey-smelling moor.

Dairy Cow's Farewell

We met our nearest neighbour on the way home from market where he'd been selling his dairy cow. No, he was not going to replace her; instead he was going to come down to our level and buy milk once or twice a week and store it in the fridge.

Farewell to the inexorable chore that made you scramble home from mirth and mart on time; farewell to the fetter that tied you by the leg to the farm; farewell to the institution that made you rise at seven instead of half-past six on a Sunday morning, thereby bamboozling yourself into believing you were leading a life of indolence and ease.

* * *

Hardly any farmer on the milk marketeer's direct route now keeps a dairy cow for his own or his workers' convenience. It is more acceptable to collect the pint bottles at the road end. Here, where we are too isolated to make a milk delivery profitable we have evolved the town dairy and fridge technique. No longer, then, in either plain or hill will Mary call "Proo-ay! Proo-ay!" to the cattle across whatever may be the local equivalent of the sands of Dee. No longer will she thrust her head against a gentle flank while her fingers coax the milk to sing its thin song against the metal pail and the cats sit in a velvet circle soliciting a fill for their old wooden "coggie."

Long ago when the timber camps for whom we supplies milk during the war years vanished we were left with a number of hand-milked dairy cows. At that time it was quite a useful proposition to go on milking them and cog dairy heifer calves on the milk. As the cows would give around six gallons of milk even on our Spartan rations and the calves needed but one, it was clear that one could rear quite a number of calves per cow. It was a cheap and quick way of getting up a stock if you did not mind the drudgery of milking times nor the fash of scouring milk pails.

* * *

Though I should not care to go back to such a policy after the ease of one beef cow to one beef calf, the calf to do its own milking, the system had is compensations. Certainly I never did make up my mind whether it was better to milk before or after supper in the long grim winters of this upland place, but there was no doubt about the pleasures of the byre once you got there.

We had pressure lanterns in those days and felt very modern and up to date and far removed from the old reeky peters of pre-war. In the light of the new lanterns the byre looked a very cheery place. The cows would look over the partitions of their stalls and watch their turn for a titbit. There was the soft rustle of bedding straw and the tiny musical clink of neck chains. On a cold night you could cuddle up to a nice, kind cow and milk away, soothed and warm, as if the storm without had nothing to do with the small security inside the thick claybiggened walls.

That is a story nearly 20 years old now and we have come a long way since then. We did not in those days know the meaning of man hours, or woman hours either. We had never heard of the subtleties of time and motion. Now we can swap the scientific jargon of the day with the best of them; and when you come to tea with me I'll fill the milk jug clean and handy from the pint bottle in the fridge. It is sad there should be something missing.

No Man's Land

Round the edges of the parks in this upland place there are man-made murrains of stones and boulders which were gathered by our predecessors when they toiled to wring these acres from the grudging moor.

Now the tumbled heaps of rocks – no man's land – lie just beyond our fences, bound together here and there with the tough natural herbage of the region, though their bleached and arid skeletons will remain forever visible, a Spartan memorial to the time when the people here won their bread in the sweat of their brow and back-breaking toil.

Not all these patches of scrub-tied gneiss are as useless as they may first appear. Sometimes it might happen that a particularly harsh and unmanageable outcrop might occur in the middle of useful enough ground. Then it was easier to cart the heaps of stones on to this rather than hump them out to the farthest boundary. Soon a sizable hillock was created where birches were swift to take root.

The farmer who had been lamenting the intransigence of the rocky islet bang in the centre of his arable found to his gratified surprise that he now had a spot which would make an acceptable shade for his beasts in summer and a welcome bield for them in winter.

Trees are not the only squatters in such outcrops. Wild flowers can infiltrate as well, and minute plants like tormentil and eyebright find hospitality and sustenance in the most unlikely granite clefts. Milkwort and trefoil soon follow, and when the farmer comes to sow his compound manure on the park proper, he finds this flowery place as good a spot as any in which to jack up his trailer load of fertiliser.

In this way the chance sown garden wins an unexpected bonus from the frills and spills of the manure bags.

We have such a patch in the hill field next the moor. We have drained the field and limed it, as well as applying to it all the knowledge and money of which we are master. The result is good and the ground grows sizable tonnages of properly constituted green fodder; but when we put the beasts in to graze behind the electric fence they find their sweetest eating, their kindest ease, among the wild flowers.

* * *

Here in the valley of the Dorbach we are accustomed to the idea of unused bits and pieces of land for the Dorbach flows into the Divie and the Divie into the Findhorn which runs through one of the oldest inhabited river valleys in the north. From time immemorial men have lived and cultivated, hunted and died along these banks. They have left their traces in their cairns and stone circles, their forts and beacons.

Although avarice stimulated by tales of buried treasure has caused many of these sites to be rifled and their boundaries dispersed, a certain underlying decency and piety forbids too wholesale a desecration.

Besides we remember with a shudder what happened when a green mound in the policies of a local estate was investigated. That turned out to be a grave containing the five headless bodies of those Cummings who waged barbarous war against Randolph Earl of Moray.

Deep Cunning of Dumb Animals

Last Friday morning, Elsie, a large red cow with a suspicious nature and a taste for the wide open spaces, went off to the hill to have her calf. Cows, generally, show a nice sense of privacy in this matter and, while we were getting ready to go to town, we could see Elsie on the other side of the burn, casting wary glances to measure just how concealed she was, not only from us but from the rest of the herd. She is an experienced mother so we had no scruples in leaving her to get on with the job and we had reasonable hopes that when we got back in the late afternoon she would have had her calf and rejoined the herd.

No Sign

When we returned after five o' clock there was no sign of her. We took field glasses and then the telescope to scan the hill but we had no success. It is no light undertaking to traipse over 800 acres of hill looking for a calf. However, it was a "beauteous evening, calm and free" though we did not feel particularly Wordsworthian at the prospect of raking over grassy knolls and heathery patches strewn with granite boulders left there by the ice age to trip the unwary.

But after all we are not exactly new to searching for calves. Perhaps you do not think a calf an easy thing to hide. Maybe you think he hits you in the eye. Then you have never had to deal with the deep cunning even the dumbest bovine shows when she conceals her young. She is adept at the secretest place. And anyway, a new-born calf is very small; a strong man can easily carry him in his oxter: indeed many's the calf Dod has carried home just like that across the burn. The calfie wriggles a bit but he is not the hazard, but his mother who comes snorting threats at your back and trying to puncture your lumbar regions with her horns.

Some cows not only hide their young but actually take them into the plot by telling them not to utter a word nor twitch an ear till mother returns. We have an Ayrshire who does this, and, if you are careful you can catch her chivvying her calf into its hide and whispering to it that she won't be long but he is to lie as quiet as quiet. Nor does that calf move a muscle till Ma returns from the byre where she has been keeping up her strength stealing cake out of other cows' troughs. Then he utters a small cry and bravely gets to his wavering wobbly legs and staggers off to his mother.

Efficient

Usually cows are very efficient about having their young and we do not worry overmuch about them. But a heifer with her first calf is different. We do not like to intrude but we do like to hover. Some behave quite trustingly but others take a malicious delight in hauling us out of bed for no reason and then after a week of broken and fractious slumber we go out to the byre to find a nice bouncing calf – all of her own work.

Gently

We once had a heifer called Megs who had been a petted indulged calf when young. When she came to have her calf she howled blue murder and insisted we should remain on call the whole time.

When it was all over we were quite exhausted and Meg was ready for a nice bran mash.

The nicest way of finding calves is to get them in the byre all warm and cuddled up to their mothers who speak to them so gently you can hardly believe it was the same cow who bellowed so fiercely at you yesterday when you fell out with her over a matter of extra potatoes. We did not find Elsie's calf till the next day because he was not born till then. She still has not taken him home but keeps him in the rashes by the old well. It's enough to give him rheumatics but Elsie says no.

26th May - 1962

Eviction Order

The week before last found me involved in one of the most melancholy duties that fall to the lot of the local busybody – that of being chairman at still another meeting about the closing of yet another rural school.

I have no words to express the mingled feelings of frustration and despair that overwhelm me at such times; and seeing the anxious rosy faces of parents filing into the schoolroom to take their places in their childrens' desks hardly helps to make endearing the brief cases and official suitings of those who take up their position in chairs behind the dominie's rostrum.

Authority reasons that I ought to preside because, being the school convener, my presence will be reassuring to the audience. Privately I think I am where I am because Authority hopes I shall be able to prevent mayhem by the fathers and mothers.

So we start off the same dreary old balance-sheet. Debits first; falling numbers, difficulty of bringing school up to code standard, difficulty of finding staff in such remote regions. Credits; the children will do so much better in a bigger school, where instead of the teacher having to cope with numerous small classes all at different stages she will have one class all at the same stage. The competitive element will brighten up every child's wits, so that there will be a huge increase in pupils able to pass into the "A" stream at the academy, at whose further goal the university – alma mater – beckons home with welcoming arms her studious sons and daughters.

The way to this impressive bourne is to make gay with music and dancing supplied by travelling specialists, who could not possibly be expected to journey up here by Randolph's fabled bridge, where Sir Andrew Moray said his prayers before leading his army safely past the English noses of Edward III's army hot-foot from subduing Lochindorb Castle. Officialdom answers in an afterthought that, of course, transport will be provided for the pupils who are to be evicted from the school. Meeting open for questions.

The parents rise on a single furious roar. They like the education their children now receive. Did the higher-ups mention science as a subject in the new streamlined school? "Practical science" is the pacifying answer, science which would help the pupil to understand how to mend a fuse and how the TV works. The thought of a 10-year-old guttering in the inside of the rented TV is too much for the parents, who indicate their abusive feelings in no uncertain manner.

The audience demands gold plated safety precautions for transporting the five to sevens.

You realise that the parents see the child as a social being, officials as a creature existing in a class room from nine till four. But despairingly you go on clearing a silence for the speakers.

The meeting ends with the parents resolving on an appeal to Mr Maclay as they hurtle in their cars over the Findhorn where the river wages its tumultuous battle with its grim environment.

Brutes with Character

Last night we let 14 stirk beasts up round the garden fence to tidy up the rough bits of grazing which in a place like this are such savers on the expensively cultivated grass in the parks.

A change of scene and pasture always excites this unlikeable gang of cattle who prefer to spend in mischief the hours their more amenable brethren pass peaceably chewing the cud. Action, not rumination, would seem their motto as they push open forbidden doors and shove destructive noses into feeding troughs not meant for them. Between times they scrap among themselves. Two big Friesians begin and soon the whole 14 are involved. All in all they show the exact reactions of any band of well-fed hoodlums with time on their hands.

It is easy to sneer at the habit of attributing to dumb brutes the emotions and thoughts supposed to belong exclusively to the superior human being. And it is a cynical fact of life that the dear little bunny is not a dear little thing by any standards. But to go all out and deny that beasts have characters is plain silly, as anyone who makes his living trafficking among them knows full well.

Any dairyman who wants to emerge in one piece at the end of his day's work knows that an Ayrshire bull must be treated with respect. He also knows that if he is to make the most of his milk bonus he must be aware of the personal idiosyncracies of his cows. It is not just whimsy that puts the record player in the milking parlour.

All breeds of cattle have their own particular likes and dislikes, their habits, and their faults. Black bulls are noted for being the most docile of all bulls, but it is wise not to presume too far on their equanimity. They can think up grievances just as foolishly and as dangerously as you can.

In the next farm but one the farmer runs two bulls, a Shorthorn and a Black. At the annual tuberculin test both bulls were taken along and subjected to the same treatment as the rest of the herd. The Shorthorn submitted with a fairly good grace but the Black took umbrage at the vet, who was wearing a black oilskin coat.

Bull also said the cattle crush was horrible and as for the injection he gave a snort by snort imitation of the Spanish bullring at its most dramatic. His owner imagined that he'd forget about the experience, but a week later the tractorman turned up for work wearing a black oilskin coat, and the bull, recollecting his humiliation and pain, made for the man.

Mercifully the employee was young and slamp and escaped with nothing worse than a fright. Eventually the bull was lent to us, and a nicer chap about the place you could not wish. He liked to accompany us on a quiet stroll about the farm, making gruffly pleasant comments on life as he found it. He was patient with the calves, tactful with his wives, and rolled down any fence that happened to impede his purpose in the most good-natured way.

We parted on happy terms, for we had the sense to remember his feelings about black oilskins.

9th June – 1962

When One's Company

There is only one reliably sheltered place in all our upland acres, the neuk made by the garage abutting on the south facing gable of the house. Here you may sit, except for the storm and drift of mid-winter, at any time of the year and enjoy some leisure.

You do not need anyone to keep you company, for after adjusting your chair to avoid the rake and hoe I am too lazy to put in their proper places, you will find, if you have eyes and ears and nose, the whole countryside ready to beguile the hour.

Straight in front of you is the old drystane dyke that once contained the kitchen garden of the old house now so ignominiously turned into a cattle fold, with its enamelled bath become a drinking trough for thirsty beeves. Three gean trees grow out of the lichened collapsing stones and make a home for our pair of bull-finches.

* * *

When you sit alone and still on an evening in early June they will come quite close, regarding you as merely another piece of landscape. They are full of small chinking commonplaces which they relay between themselves in the most companionable manner possible. While they comment on the possibilities of a gooseberry bush a bellow from the steading disconcerts them and they fly off; and you reflect that Wee Cow has lost her calf yet again.

Wee Cow is one of those girl mothers so agitating to social workers, but she is a devoted parent. It is a pity that Wee Calf is so correspondingly minute that when she falls asleep behind a dandelion Wee Cow cannot see her. But the bellow will awake the sleeper and there will be a beautiful reunion such as you have already witnessed dozens of times.

Your imagination leaves mother and child to it, for already there is a pulverising sound on the summer air. The big buses are changing gear at the foot of the hill that leads on past your road end up to Grantown. These buses are full of airmen from Kinloss going on leave. It is much more convenient to charter a bus than wait for the timetables and connections that are the fate of travellers going south by British Railways.

Where the buses change gear the road is a bare 16ft. wide, and we never cease wondering how heavy goods traffic negotiates all its hazards. But it does. It is only the private driver on his way home from a dance in the early hours of Saturday morning who muffs things.

Last Saturday we were astonished to find a car in the middle of one of our fields. We were glad no one was injured but exasperated to discover that we must once more take up our summer job of mending a fence burst by another motorist.

You are enjoying your own company too much to warp the moment working out in £ s d what new posts and droppers are going to cost for 70 yards of ruined fence. Summer breathes enchantingly from primula and pansy. Noses are pleasant in the country where every season has its appropriate fragrance. Birch is sticky sweet in spring; clover sleepy and syrupy in summer; heather, honey hot in autumn; and pines are clean and cold all the long winter. What a fascinating world a dog must inhabit. Or does he? Here comes Bob the collie laughing all over. He smells disgustingly. One's company no longer.

16th June - 1962

Old School Ties

We are in this parish much bewildered by the fortunes of one of our three remaining country schools. Will it close this year, next year, sometime, never? While I worry over its predicament I cannot but reflect ruefully that each time I find myself involved in the fortunes of one of these admirable institutions it seems to signify the kiss of death as far as they are concerned.

Not only have I been in on the obsequies of two of them but I even have the mouldering remains of another on this very farm. Every time we go to look at the cattle summering on the hill we pass the tumbled boulders that were once its walls, and see the dim grass-grown outline of its foundations.

* * *

In 1793 there were 1800 people in the glen which was served by two schools. One of them was the parish school where the dominie was paid £5 8s 4d per annum for teaching 30 pupils the three Rs. The second school was in another part of the glen called Relugas and there the establishment was conducted with the support of the Society for the Propagation of Christian Knowledge.

The society had been encouraged in this project by a gift of £261 13s 7d sent them by Dr Duncan Cumming, son of the Laird of Relugas. Duncan was physician to William III and after the Battle of the Boyne settled in Dublin where he seems to have prospered, if one goes by such a handsome donation to the parish of his birth.

The Relugas Cummings were always anxious for the general improvement of the district and one of them imported Alexander Wilson from Berwickshire in 1798 whose function it was to give the place a new look – which Alexander did so successfully that, when he died, five extensive and respectable proprietors clubbed together to do his memory proud with a marble tablet in the kirk-yard honouring "his zeal and fidelity in the management of the estates in the neighbourhood."

What with liming and farming and landscape gardening on a vast scale Alexander had not much time over to organize the formal schooling of the pupils in the parish. But improvement was in the air and by 1842 there were five schools though the population had fallen from 1800 to 1123.

One of these schools was my ruined school on the green knoll by the banks of the little burn. It was a female school and 30 pupils attended it. The teacher was paid "on her own adventure." Was adventure a paying spec 120 years ago? And how did it compare in terms of cash with the settled salary of the parish schoolmaster at a maximum of £34 4s 4d?

* * *

My adventurous headmistress was of course not eligible for the bequest of Mr Dick whose trustees paid £38 5s 1d to augment the schoolmaster's wage. But if you notice that £16 was the sum paid in fees at the parish school, and this came from 60 pupils, it is easy enough to work out that our headmistress with exactly half that number of children would have netted the large sum of £8 a year. Even with hens at sixpence each in Forres and eggs at three half-pence a dozen I doubt if adventure paid off.

No one now knows what she taught though it would be safe to assume that spinning would have been an important subject since for long the women of the parish were notable for their skill in this. But all is conjecture. The school died and the wind whistles in the rigging of the pylons the hydro board have erected above its turfy playground.

23rd June - 1962

Destructive and Elegant

This week-end we have some Girl Guides in residence. They are trying their campers' badge and permit and have pitched their tents in the narrow grassy enclosure between the gable of the old house and the thick fir planting which we hope will afford them some shelter from the hacking wind of upland June.

We are quite used to having such camps through the summer and know better than to offer advice or help to damsels as efficient and independent as these. However, this time we thought it might be in order for us to warn them not to be afraid when they heard loud guttural barking at midnight from the depths of the forest.

It was not the Hound of the Baskerville's giving tongue but roe deer admonishing their young and shouting defiance to any would-be molesters. The girls were delighted with the information and now are all agog to see Bambi come stepping delicately through the trees. We'll feel shockingly remiss if he does not materialise.

Since this district was planted seven years ago the trees have flourished amazingly, and now stand in great impenetrable shelters across moor and Knock. As they have grown, so has the roe deer population, who find sanctuary and food among the thick-set pine. Anxious foresters wage unceasing war on them, for they are as destructive as elegant, and in winter hardly a week goes by without a roe hunt being organized on some estate in the neighbourhood.

Roe, unlike the red deer who live and move in herds, lead rather aloof lives. We can see them eating their solitary breakfasts in the field we mean to cut for hay, or bounding with their mate in spectacular aerial leaps across the hill. With their long, slim legs and delicately set head and shoulders they seem more birds than beasts, and they move with a similar delicious lightness.

* * *

In spite of their apparent shyness they are self-possessed creatures, and when we come on them at their illicit browsing, all they do is lift their heads and give us mild reproachful stares as if we were the trespassers, not they. They rather trade on this, and when one of them took up residence over the gate from our neighbour who had evolved with slavish labour a garden out of boulder and peat, she felt honoured.

Even after the roe had eaten her brussel sprouts she seemed to lack the moral energy to see the matter for what it was – namely, a case of impudent theft. Instead she remained hypnotised by the creature's ruthless charm. However now that summer is here with the lettuces, she does begin to wonder if the roe is not overdoing it by bringing along his wife and child. But it will take more than an irate female gardener to shift the roe deer family. The doe is especially determined and courageous.

* * *

One of our friends here has a white cat who chooses to bring up her kittens in a woody bank near the farm. A roe deer happened to drop her calf in this vicinity, and while she was recovering from the pangs of motherhood Puss was returning from the farm kitchen. The deer, seeing her, at once gave chase with every symptom of vicious reprisal. The cat fled through the undergrowth with the deer in furious pursuit.

Mercifully for Puss there was a tree up which she swarmed with the speed of light and there she remained fill the deer, satisfied that she had routed the enemy, returned to her calf who had scrambled on to his reed-thin legs and was emitting shrill cries like an owlet before a storm.

Summer Outings

The season of the summer outing is upon us, and even if we do live in the depths of the country, we are no more immune to its rigours than our cousins living within the walls of cities.

On the appropriate occasions we, too, must up and go, for reasons as social as enjoyable. In other districts the theme of the summer excursion is capable of infinitely charming variety; it can vary from the sophistication of the *son et lumière* to the salty merriments of steaming round Highland lochs. Here, where we neighbour the foothills of the Cairngorms, our choice is much more restricted. If you leave out the local cattle show, which anyway is six weeks off, you are left with the "Big Hoose" garden and the Rural expedition. For both you have to be in pretty good physical condition, though the "Big Hoose" does not call for quite the same stamina as the Rural junketing.

If you go with the Rural you will find yourself embarked on an adventure which will hurl you in a bus across Scotland at its widest and will presuppose that you can keep going buoyantly from one dawn till the next. You must be able to rise above travel sickness and indigestion tablets; nor should your passion for scenery be so strong that you will resent steamed up bus windows streaked with rain instead of views of waterfalls and deep romantic chasms.

No wonder the less robust of us opt for the "Big Hoose" garden. Scotland's Gardens Scheme, to give it its party name, aims, by opening private gardens to the public, at augmenting the funds of various charities, of which the chief is the benevolent fund of the Scottish District Nurses. There are other good causes, too, but the one that registers with us is nursing.

The district nurse is easily the most popular necessity in any rural community. She is loved for the immediate and urgent service she does us; but she is also revered since she never abuses her vast power. Insensibly she has come to assume for us some of the significance of the parson and the doctor.

* * *

For all these reasons we do not grudge getting into gumboots and waterproofs on a June afternoon when the wind is in the east and the rain comes belting up from the Firth to go and pay our shillings at the gate of the "Big Hoose" garden.

The larches turn up their heavy green fur collars against the cold and the gale runs through the beech like a burn in spate. The herbaceous borders shed disintegrating petals before the onslaughts of an upland summer and the rose garden sullenly refuses to unfurl its buds under the gun-metal sky.

There are damp afternoon teas served in the old laundry where card tables are covered with drawing-pinned white shelf paper and enthusiastic Girl Guides wash up. The Calor Gas stove specially imported hisses gallantly beneath urns that have no intention of boiling.

Such a pity the season is so late. There are no soft fruits for sale this year. So sad the winter slew the lilies. Where did I leave my umbrella?

In the gable of our parish kirk there is an old cracked marble tablet to the memory of Alexander Wilson, who was our local equivalent of Capability Brown, the great eighteenth-century landscape gardener. An old-fashioned pink rose runs sweetly riot over his grave and I wonder what he would have thought of our summer excursions to the gardens he laid out all these years ago. He would not have known about the charities, but he would have known about the weather.

Prize-Giving Time

Owing to complications arising from the altered date of the new leaving certificates, we find ourselves cluttered with prize days when the rest of Scottish schools have already written a neat finish to session 1961-62.

Though our three small country schools are aggrieved at being still at lessons when everyone else is on holiday, no one is unduly cast down, for the ends of our summer terms have always been treated with cheerful nonchalance.

We have never needed to embark on onerous arrangements involving hiring picture-house auditoriums to accommodate parents and pupils and we have not had to scramble about looking for a suitable speaker.

Each school copes in its own way with the ordeal. One runs it in connection with a concert-cum-ceilidh; another amalgamates it with the annual school picnic to the shore, while the smallest puts on a wild flower display before awarding every single pupil a picture book.

Though all three schools have an official closing date it does not follow that they have their festivity on that date. This year, for instance, the concert-cum-ceilidh school is first on the timetable. The dominie, as you will have guessed, is a Celt, and in moments of emotion reverts to his native Gaelic.

Because he has the casual habit of social ease belonging to his people, his party gets off to an intimate start with mothers chatting cheerfully as they wander among the tables where examples of the pupils' handiwork is on show. There are cups of tea and Gaelic songs and such an air of relaxed informality that the outsider gets a shock when the incredibly good results of the eleven plus are read out in a gentle self-effacing Highland voice.

The picnic prize day is quite different. It had its origins in the days when, because of lack of communications, it was difficult for parents to get together very often. But it was so successful that the arrangement has continued. There seems to be something special about a prize given out at the seaside. As like as not while the bookish is being handed his reward the practical is hauling a baby out of the paddling-pool where the silly little creature has dived in head first.

The acclaim which follows this sensible action makes up for the lack of academic recognition. While the baby licks an ice-cream cone between salty hiccups, we all stand round agreeing that book learning is not everything.

Finally there is the flower-show prize day. Of all the functions this is the only one that really takes place on the closing day. Glass jam jars crammed with trefoil and forget-me-not stand round the wide window ledges and unnaturally tidy infants prink in newly cleaned desks. There is no avant-garde flower arrangement here – the more flowers to the jar the better.

One has, therefore, to keep an eagle eye on Johnny lest he pinch Ellie's windflowers, while Ellie is not above stretching out a predatory paw in the direction of Norman's winter green.

Because of an endowment left over from an age when there were many more pupils at this school, there is now enough money to give each child a prize. This comfortable arrangement which makes all feel clever and successful is one I could recommend to any school. It is quite the best way to begin any holiday.

14th July - 1962

Hay-Making Time

In early July we are obsessed with the necessity of getting the hay made and baled before the Glasgow trades weeks get properly under way since so often their advent ushers in a fortnight's drenching rain.

Every time we see a thundery cloud welling up out of the hills we cast an anguished look at the calendar and pray that the threat will pass. It looks as if our supplications will be answered and by the time the first bus load of trippers make our isolated hinterland most of the bales will be safely stored in barn and shed.

Although the silage pit has taken much of the headache out of haymaking, in that if offers a method of conserving grass independent of the tantrums of a Scottish summer, we'd all prefer to make hay if we could. Certainly silage is both palatable and nutritious but it is not so neatly handled. "You can't feed silage out of the boot of your car," a neighbour said, summing up the difference – a remark more comprehensible to the agriculturally minded than to the normal citizen who uses his car for the purposes intended by its maker, instead of for careering over the fields with fodder aboard for outwintering herds.

* * *

Before the college boys got hold of us to initiate us into the mysteries of grass growing and management, haymaking was one of our more picturesque if primitive farming operations. In the little irregular fields which slope from hill to burn, men and women, straw-hatted, sun-bonneted, used to turn out in great numbers. They carried the simple implements of the time, wooden rakes and forks. Some very advanced farms had horse-drawn mowers but in others the scythe was more commonly used.

A pleasant picnic air predominated. There were jugs of home-made beer and baskets full of girdle scones thickly spread with crowdie for the sustenance of the labourers. Nobody knew about balanced grass-seed mixtures, while the idea of fertilising for a second cut would have been treated with the tolerant amusement reserved for infant babblings. Now we can all chat knowledgeably about chemical percentages in artificial manure and tetraploid strains in new grasses. It's a pity there are so few of us left thus to chat.

* * *

As the growing of hay has improved so has its making. Down in the Laich, where it is reckoned a cash crop, it is treated with the mechanised respect due to a valuable commodity. In the fat low fields of Alves and Duffus you can see the tractors, the mowers, the crimpers, the rakes, and the balers all at work under the blue sky. If you are arithmetically minded you can work out how many hundreds of pounds all the equipment costs and try equating it with the massive tonnage it is securing, all at £13 a ton ex field.

People like myself who come from the bare uplands gaze hungrily and enviously at the abundance so effortlessly produced. What astronomic number of hill cows could we not keep if we had fields capable of producing these great sweet knee-high swathes we see stretching for acre after acre? We try to comfort ourselves by recollecting that our country grows more sheep than cattle and sheep do not care for long heavy hay, preferring short easily nibbled stuff. But we have to work hard to persuade ourselves.

Pussyfooting for Supper

In addition to Smiler, who is the house cat, we have four cats who live in the barn – Fluff, Smoke, Torty-Tab, and Charley. They are fed once a day with porridge and milk, plus Smiler's left-overs, which are quite considerable since her minute appetite can tolerate only freshly cooked sole and raw steak mince that has not been in the fridge a moment over eight hours.

The barn cats, in return for their meal, lead a life devoted to the sacred business of catching mice and rats. In their off-duty hours they lie around on the top of our expensively dried grass which fills the barn to overflowing with its green brittle sweetness. All they ask of humans, in addition to their porridge plus, is that we should be content with the stations which cats have allotted to us. Familiarity is not to be permitted. At least not till the other evening.

The hour was still fairly early, just after the supper dishes had been washed, when Charley appeared in the garden. His waist-coat was a sparkling white, his grey coat newly home from the tailors. Surprisingly he did not carry a topper to match. He stood by the rhododendron and when he had successfully collected all human eyes he moved over to the mole heaps beyond and began to dance.

All the time he danced, out-Bolshoi-ing every Russian ballet dancer ever born, his green eyes glowed. Beneath his velvet tread the blind moles scurried down their cold subterranean corridors, not so panic-stricken, I was exasperated to note, that they were not able to avoid the traps I had set to murder them in revenge for the evil they have done to my lawn.

* * *

We were amused and puzzled by the performances and were about to put it down to another feline incomprehensibility when there was a scuffling at the back door. When we opened it, there was Charley with Torty-Tab on his arm. As plain as anything he said, "My wife, poor woman, is starving. See for yourselves how thin and worn she is. Pay me for the dance by feeding her. Please, good kind sirs."

Hurriedly I flew round getting sustenance for the poor woman – I mean cat. One is apt to get confused at times especially when one recollects, as I did, the tinker piper who used to play this very trick upon soft-hearted country-women when I was a girl. Humbly I proffered a bowl of warm food to Torty who accepted it in a frail but gracious manner. Charley stood blandly by as complacent as he could look about the kittens which he knew, and I knew, and Torty knew were securely hidden in the barn.

When she had finished Charley smelled the bowl carefully but there was not a pick of food remaining. He asked Torty if she thought she could walk to the barn with his aid. So they departed. Charley is a better performer than the tinker, Torty is a sight cleaner than the tinker woman, but the nub of the situation is exactly the same. How upsetting if there were something in reincarnation.

Crystal Gazing Studio

When we, who live near Forres, want to buy a wedding present that has to be special and different we know exactly where to go. We set out immediately for the studio where we can choose a set of virgin crystal and have it engraved with the design of our choice or invention.

The studio stands gable end on to a road that goes nowhere in particular and swags of clematis grow up to its windows. It has a daffodil yellow door and a latch that is old-fashioned without being mannered. Inside it is divided into two rooms – one a storeroom where the glass lives in cupboards, the other the workroom with the huge bank of engraving drills in the window.

The store has every kind of glass you can imagine. Most of it is bright pure Edinburgh crystal, but there is foreign stuff, too. The Swedes, who have the secret of how to make solidity translucent, send smooth oblongs that become vases and ornaments cold and clear as the icicles that are their essence.

In a dark corner you may glimpse an old claret decanter, pouting and sloping shouldered as an eighteenth-century beauty in a harem-line gown. We do not drink decanted claret any longer because the process takes too long. If you are a claret drinker today you must finish the bottle at one sitting since tomorrow it is sour, so I am told.

There is nothing arty about this studio. Local people drop out and in to admire the glasses destined for a local aristocratic house with a pedigree longer than royalty's; more folk come in to hope that the set of goblets bought by the Government for our Comrade in Russia will fill him with the friendly feelings our Scottish way-side flowers so magically incised on the sides of the glasses must arouse.

The more we crystal-gaze, the more fascinated we become. Will the artist really do us sherry glasses for us alone with our very own name on them? He says he will. But he is firm. There must be no question of us ultimately knowing better than him. No, he will not engrave a squat Aberdeen-Angus bull on any jug, glass, or carafe even if it did win a first prize at Grantown or Smithfield.

* * *

Not but what the artist thinks he is a very fine bull, but his place of remembrance is on a photograph, not on a fragile convex of glass. Now, if he looked like these: the artist points out a pencil sketch of the sculptured bulls of Burghead with their lovely flowing Mithraic lines. Exasperated we point out that these bulls are no known breed and would never get a prize. "Ach," says the artist, who is a local man and knows his lore. "It's a cross Shorthorn, that one. What are you blethering about?"

If he is firm with his designs, he is also firm about his customers. He must know each individually. This throws middle-men who have seen his work at international exhibitions into a tizzy of fury. But he remains firm, the communication that must exist between the artist and his audience is not to be tampered with.

Orders accomplished, bubbles made palpable, stand ready to be packed. A little girl's name runs round the rim of a goblet, words to the music lying in the cup eager to escape at the touch of a finger.

Fun with a Float

One of the worst headaches afflicting promoters of the local one-day agricultural show is caused by the difficulty they have in providing suitable entertainment for their afternoon spectators.

The morning is easy, for the drama and tension that accompany the judging of stock and home-crafts is such that everyone is on tip-toe with excitement. But when the glittering cups are awarded, the rosettes pinned up, the claret and blue certificates of merit propped up against the appropriate scones and hand-knitted baby jackets, a blank reaction may set in, which, if not dealt with crisply from the outset, may slide the whole affair into the bog of boredom.

That is why haggard secretaries try to arrange programmes of horse racing and show jumping. If they are lucky they contact a co-operative military band or a roar of trick motor-cyclists. But if they are sensible they opt out and hand over to the Rural.

The Rural have an invariable and triumphant answer to the dilemma. They put on the spectacle of the decorated float – or floats. The float is, of course, the tableau vivant on wheels. It has been sure-fire entertainment since the Elizabethan trade guilds used it for portraying bits and pieces of the Bible story to the groundlings of their crowded towns. It remains an integral part to-day of the Lord Mayor's Show in London. In the hands of the Rural it has gained in ingenuity while losing nothing of its pristine gaiety.

No one would be foolish enough to believe that there are no snags connected with the project even with the Rural members all doing their best. The country family out for the afternoon have clear ideas about what they want to watch. The show must be about something familiar; it must be presented in an original way, and its end-product must be loud uninhibited laughter.

So that brings the Rural bang up against the theme they wish to present. Obviously it must be something to do with farming. But it must not be too technical. We do not, while licking a stick of candyfloss, wish to follow the intricacies of administering vaccine to poultry likely to take fowl pest. Something like the farm kitchen from Pict to spin-dryer is more in our line. Nothing then delights us more than to recognize the participants in the tableau, be they never so thoroughly disguised in their grannies' petticoats or their daughters' tightest jeans.

Elevated on a float away from the frustrations of everyday convention the shyest woman loses her self-consciousness. "Kilting her coats" like Leezie Lindsay, she tramps blankets in a wooden tub while the latest detergents sends up a lather of bubbles that would have been the envy of our mothers. Gaily she kicks footfuls of soapy water at the audience while the float lurches round the tree-framed arena.

Some one else holds up the ample intimate garments of a generation that knew flannel and feather-stitching rather than nylon and drip dry. Gales of laughter follow the float's progress and the hour flits past in that mood of rustic good nature which is the test of the successful show.

Lammas Deluge

At such a moment, with the Twelfth standing in the wings, we should be pleasurably agog with hope for a good sporting week, a fitting opening to an exuberant Highland Season.

Instead, we are running about as nimbly as gum boots and oilskins will allow, ordering treacle for a silage pit kept by the continual rain at a shockingly high temperature, and wondering desperately whether the new mouth the county council have cut for the Spey will do what is asked for. We are certainly having more than enough water to scour out the fresh channel the villagers, in historic Kingston at the mouth of the river, hope will relieve them from the perpetual threat of being washed away.

Morayshire has always been vulnerable to Lammas deluges, of which the most notorious was the 1829 flood, later elevated into a minor topographical classic and an awful warning of what rivers in North-East Scotland can do, by Sir Thomas Dick Lauder.

At that time the farms bordering the Dorback – of which we are one – suffered severe loss not only in the more immediate ways of stock and crop but in the very fields themselves. The soil in these had become so spongy with the steady rain that the flooded river was able to gouge them from their foundations and send them weltering downstream. A bank a hundred feet high with slopes and terraces covered in birch and alder fell, as the then tenant of a neighbouring farm said, "wi' a sort of dumb sound." And as he watched appalled half an acre more followed, so that the unfortunate farmer began to think he would soon see his whole farm disintegrate by fields and go sailing to the sea.

But it does not take a disaster on the 1829 scale to carve out new aspects on an old scene. Five years ago we had torrential rain about this time. Every burn and river in upland Moray filled with thundering spate and surged down to the plain; the Scottish Office had an enormous bill to foot for repairing the damage. Here where we have raw sandy cliffs, bitter legacy from the earlier flood, the river Dorback undermined their foundations which crumbled with a kind of sick celerity and dyed the water an ugly milky colour for miles downstream.

* * *

We are making silage from the grass in the fields bordering the cliffs and naturally enough do not care to send the forage harvester too near the lips of these gaunt uneasy heights. Down in the valley on a spit of meadow a party of Scouts have erected a tent – a brave though foolish gesture and one my middle-aged soul deprecates. I'd much rather they'd go home to their nice dry homes in Forres where their anxious mothers are waiting with dry clothes and large hot meals not concocted out of tins.

Still I suppose the grouse are bearing up. For them it may be glorious enough.

Fending off the Raiders from the Hills

After the first cut of hay came off the old barley park, away back in June, the field got a suitable dressing of fertiliser and now shines out verdant and lush as if it were spring.

Seeing its appetising appearance from afar the hill cows have descended and stand pressing their greedy noses against the barrier fence much as bairns do outside a sweetie shop. One gets inured to such pleading but there comes a day when the wind feels more than usually inhospitable and one begins to think that perhaps there may be something to be said for putting the beasts on to fresh pasture.

Come another month the calf sales will be on us and forward calves with a chip on them are more likely to meet a ready market than others who will need a long store period before coming to cash.

So we go to look at the hill. The cows think that we have at last relented and congregate excitedly at the hill gate. They intimate they are thankful that we agree that keep is getting tight. What can you expect with August half gone? We reply that it is a long, long time to spring and surely there is something to be said for a back-end spent strip-grazing. Why, we might not have to open the silage till after Christmas!

There are no signs of enthusiasm at this thrifty prospect. Instead a good deal of grumbling is heard in the back row about what happened last year when the first snow came in November and by the middle of December, we were all – beast, human, and grass – buried deep in winter waste. A fat lot of good strip-grazing was then. The Promised Land ought to be now.

But we are not ready to give in, and shut the gate firmly against the queue-jumpers before setting off down the peat path to the old crofts. It is comforting at last to see the heather re-establishing itself after our savage burning. There were acres of waist-high stuff some years ago and we burned the lot in what looked to everyone an orgy of incendiarism. We were not without a shiver of anxiety ourselves but the bonfire paid off. So did the miles of slavish hill drains. The bog where the rushes quaked has firmed as the water found its new channel to the burn.

* * *

About a dozen calves still feed contentedly enough on the natural herbage where once the crofts stood. They look black, bloomy fellows with the promise of growth. But the hill is not what it was. To the north a neighbouring estate has gone in for hill reclamation in a big way. If our hill looked like that we'd leave the beasts where they are. And we envy the resources we have not got.

But behind us there is a little wired-off enclosure which two seasons ago held hay bales for out-wintered beasts. The ground in the enclosure was seeded from the bales. It was protected from hares and roes, and the ground about it was trodden and fertilised by the cattle. The result is a clump of useless Yorkshire fog, a plume of fescue, and a raddled tuft of timothy.

All of which hardly adds up to good feeding or sound finance. Perhaps we are better with managed heather, clean drains, and the exquisite tapestry the modest flowers native to the hill sow indefatigably where they find a foothold.

All right, cows. Come home.

On the Gloomy Side

The farmer who wishes to lead a balanced life needs only two things, a farm and a grumble. Everybody knows this; but sometimes those who have to deal with him in a business or social way overlook the deep-seated implications and so cause themselves needless frustration.

My heart often bleeds for new young representatives of seeds firms making their initial call on the encrusted farmer. The poor lamb has a list of letters after his name, a burning faith in the product he is selling, and the foresight to have made inquiries of his elders about the most suitable hour to approach his prospective customer. So behold him, then, smilingly confident on the doorstep at 12.40 p.m., as sure of his timing as his facts.

Twenty minutes later he is still talking, stumbling a little now in his spiel as it is borne in on him that he is not making an impression, far less a sale. As he lays his list of glossy pamphlets on the sink ledge on his apologetic way out, his eyes plead spanielwise asking what he did wrong?

The answer is simple. He began with a cheery comment on the weather and the crops. This is a major gaffe. He'd have got by perhaps if he'd commented sourly on either, though it would have been so much more comfortable if he'd been gloomy about both.

The ideal approach begins with a brief resumé of the cold, droughty conditions of the spring, moves on to the unfavourable winds which have hindered growth over a wide district, and comes to a dying fall on the large quantity of laid barley consequent on the recent flood. A rather shrewd move is to imply that though the present farmer has had his fair share of such misfortunes his immediate neighbours have come off much worse.

Naturally in a district where stock is of more interest than crops the gambits are different, though the spirit infusing them is the same. The budding salesman then would be well to mug up a few dramatic facts on the growing incidence of tick in hill regions where heather-burning has been sadly neglected for some years.

* * *

Unless he really knows his veterinary stuff he is better to confine his chat to the gloomy anecdote than to the symptoms of deficiency diseases, which he may be conversant with and the farmer may not. If he can contribute a story about a tuberculin test breakdown in the next parish occasioned by a pulmonary trouble in the orraman, he will find himself on safer ground, and his prospective customer still with him.

Prices are always a safe topic. Anyone wanting to brush up on these should look in at the local mart, where the auctioneer with incredible gall refers to the farmer who is standing in the ring with his livestock as "a fine cheery seller," while the expression on the seller's face is enough to make the onlooker take to lifelong melancholia out of sympathy.

There are times when it is difficult to keep up the gloom. When the larks sing in the sweet blue sky and the silage or hay or corn is coming rolling in to its appropriate storage, being Mark Tapley in reverse makes great demands. But practice will prevent cheerfulness breaking through.

Farming on the Heather Line

Farming above the heather line forced us, some time ago, to take a long cool look at the expensive hazards of securing our cereals. The result is that for the third year running we have no conventional harvest.

We solve the winter keep difficulty by silage-making and the management of grass, so that we escape the headaches of stacks, corn, and straw. The new technique runs like this: manure for early bite and a first cut of hay; manure again for silage; manure once more for back-end strip grazing. An unexpected weather bonanza might even enable you to make some September hay. One's premium bond might come up.

* * *

But though the shift to silage has meant a great easing of the old load of anxiety, the load has not quite disappeared. The climate continues, as ever, to be capricious, and this year's seemed to reach a new record in causing exasperation. Deluges were swiftly succeeded by hot spells, which in turn gave way to whirlwinds. We could see these rising out of nowhere, bits of heather and bracken defining their otherwise invisible dimensions.

Mindless as their names, they flew over hill and burn till they came to the heavy silage crop which they took a fiendish delight in corkscrewing into such unmanageable swathes that the harvester could cut the crop on one side only – a sad and expensive waste of time.

* * *

Meanwhile black-backed gulls sat round on fences or wheeled above the pools left by yesterday's thunder plumps. They exchanged raucous reminiscences about other storms they had seen, and encouraged one another to regard the untidy sky where dirty clouds alternated with bits and pieces of rainbow that looked like chandeliers broken by an impetuous and clumsy housemaid.

In spite of a dot-and-carry procedure imposed by weather tantrums, we worked away at the home pit and got if filled easily enough. We were greatly helped because both field and pit are within the farm and we do not have to cross the main road during the operation, which we have to do down at the other place.

There farms steadings and buildings are bang on the highway. At one time the arrangement would have been convenient but not now, and not at holiday time when the traffic is unceasing. Besides, no one in a car expects farming operations to be conducted via the road. Fields are where farmers work.

But Johnny, the rangy Englishman whom we'd engaged for the duration of the silage-making, was not at all put out when he had to navigate his outfit of tractor and high forage cart into a stream of cars going in both directions on a road 16 feet wide. When Johnny had to make a sharp right turn he leaned precariously out of his clumsy caravan and grinning cheerfully would signal his intentions with an enormous hand, black with grease and honest toil.

The effect on the other drivers could hardly have been good for their blood pressure. But all the stuff is now in and Johnny, whose last job was in Dorset, indicates his intention of hanging around a while to see what happens next in heather line farming.

On Elegies in Churchyards

One of the duties of the local district council is looking after the churchyards and burial grounds within their boundaries.

The task is not onerous, for there is a list – 18 regulations long – governing the correct practices, so that when in doubt all we have to do is consult the book of words. Not that we have to do that very often, for most people inured to being pigeon-holed in life, find no difficulty in being filed for reference when dead.

Still, there are occasions when a relative wants a more liberal reading of the three inches which must separate the base of a tombstone from the edge of the lair. Then the councillor whose business it is to take an immediate and sympathetic view hies off to other older kirkyards in search of suitable precedents to reinforce the plea.

This is the most useless thing he could do, for rules and regulations even when bound in a neat wee book and signed with official seals lose their relevance when contemplated *sub specie aeternitatis*. All arrangements for turf and memorials to be placed with that geometric precision which will enable the flying squad with a motor mower to keep the dead in regimented tidiness are vain in a place where the last resting places of the forefathers of the glen jostle one another in a kindly chaos.

Roses nod affably to one another above the gravestones, people from far away come to look for the graves of their ancestors, "storied urns and animated busts" stand around in easy relaxed attitudes and overall is the gentle sociability of the remembered dead.

Forgetting the purpose of the visit, it is pleasing and tranquil to step among the epitaphs and elegies engraved on the stones. Most of them appear to have been composed by relatives anxious to pen a reference for the departed to hand over to St. Peter immediately on arrival. Others read as if the dead had not only written them but were still hovering around thinking how accurate the words continue to be.

* * *

There is the grave of "Alexander Anderson sumtym of Wester Alves, Mair of the erldom of Murray wha deit 25th Nov. 1571." Engraved on the stone are the words "fra Birt to graif, na rest we haif." The reader has an uncomfortable sense of a haggard presence beyond his shoulder.

John Geddes, the glover buried in Elgin Cathedral, would seem a brisker sould with a lively Scottish common sense:

This world is a cite full of streets
And Death the mercat all men meets.
If Lyfe were a thing that monie could buy
The poor could not live and the rich would not die.

But the elegy that intrigues me most is the one above the grave on William MacConnochie, a farmer buried in Mortlach in 1824. He rests under the sombre elegance of the last stanza of Horace's Epistle to Dellius:

Omnes eodem cogimur, omnium
versatur urna serius ocius
sors exitura et nos in aeternum
exilium inpositura cymbae.

Marsh's translation reads:

All to one fold are herded, first or last
The lot from out the shaken urn is cast
That posts each wight across the Stygian sound
For everlasting exile bound.

William disdains the translation. He can keep company with the most sophisticated pagan shades on their own terms.

Benefits or Advantages

Next week the claim for a rise in farm wages is due for consideration in England, and once more farmers and their workers on both sides of the Border will be taking a long, cool look at an industry which must have one of the most tortuous wage structures in Britain.

Roughly speaking, the farm worker is paid a wage which is made up of actual cash and "benefits or advantages" – perquisites for short. These include the tied cottage and the provision of certain foodstuffs – meal, milk, and tatties – at nominal prices. They may further mean a fixed number of free loads of firewood and an allowance for electricity. As such provisions vary from district to district and from farm to farm, no wonder attempts at rationalisation are apt to end in vertigo.

But farm wages are not the only rural emoluments to be bedevilled with the difficulty of the benefit or advantage. Gamekeepers and stalkers are equally involved, except that for them the side payments take a different form. For the farm servant's meal, milk, and tatties, read cow, suit, and dogs for the sporting employee.

Because of the difficulty of supplying the Big House with milk during the shooting season, keepers on more inaccessible moors are encouraged to keep a cow. Food for the beast comes from the croft which accompanies the shooting. The income from the milk is considered the property of the keeper's wife who also gets paid for cleaning and caretaking in the lodge.

The ubiquity of the milk marketeers has made a difference to the bargaining value of the cow in some cases and, there, cottage and hall both deal with the same firm. Suits, however, still seem a desirable part of the fee if the vision of large handsome men stepping round in identical checks "ower the moor among the heather" is anything to go by. The clothing coupon crisis dashed the suit perquisite for long, but, when it was over, estates shook their own individually designed checks from the camphor with the present pleasingly masculine results.

The last sporting perk, an allowance for dogs, never could be reckoned either a benefit or advantage for it did not come anywhere near keeping the animal – though I'm bound to say there were never any complaints and the dogs took their place with the rest of the family.

If all this looks complicated book-keeping, what about the bits and pieces that make up the pay of the aristocrat of sporting employees, the stalker? In the old days the stalker got a minute weekly wage, but as he always managed on his retirement to emerge with a bank balance in keeping with his stately bearing, one can but conclude that there must have been a pot of gold behind such unlikely subjects as cured deerskins and basins of venison fat.

A more obvious source of income was the sale of hind carcases to Germany. The hinds were shot in winter when the stalker was master of his forest and the hind venison was an important part of his perquisites. Not so important but not negligible either were the vestigial ivory tusks in the jaw of the red deer. Cuff-link manufacturers bought these.

And finally there was the tip. One never knew what form this might take when a "toff" got carried away by his imagination and it must have taken superhuman grace to look pleased at the offer of a hunting trip to India when a cash-down payment would have been so much more convenient. Still it added up over a lifetime.

Flowers, Common or Garden

If it were not blowing an icy gale I would be in the garden snipping away the tatty autumnal remains of lupins and peonies. As it is, when I'm not putting another log on the fire I'm regarding the inhospitable aspect from the warm side of the sitting-room window.

The garden here has had a raw deal from the beginning, for its foundations were laid on the old peat stack found that used to supply fuel for the original farmhouse. There is no subsoil worth mentioning, unless you can dignify the arthritic skeleton of upland Moray with that name.

The poor little patch has its moments. In spring it does itself – and me – proud by putting on a splendid show of daffodils and scyllas, primulas, and crocuses. But spring flowers do not last, and soon we are back to our regulars. These are of two kinds: those which come from a nursery and behave courageously of their own free will, and those I annex from friends which never quite forgive me for their transfer.

* * *

The brave ones are the lupins, the pyrethrums, and the opulent peonies. The last are astonishing. They were slow starters, but now they flower magnificently every year in white, scarlet, and pale pink. The only things to rival them in luxuriance are the candytufts and Siberian wallflowers. These I sowed out of a packet some years ago, and nothing can curb their high spirits.

I feel it is so noble of them to behave thus that I seldom do more than thin them out. When they plant themselves in the middle of the front path or take up untidy residence in a row against the gable which carries the kitchen fire, I leave them alone. This is a gardening attitude not really to be encouraged, for it leads to hideous results, as when an anaemic marigold coyly supports a clump of pink sea daisies or a dark red antirrhinum infiltrates into the territory annexed by the Siberian wallflowers.

The flowers I acquire behave differently. They were the popper plants a kind reader once sent me to help to combat the mole menace. They took to their surroundings with enthusiasm till the gales began whooping it up and then their heights were the death of them. I had to have them carted away. The moles were delighted and immediately moved back. I am glad to say the poppers did not die without heirs and there are lots of new baby poppers growing away like mad and getting ready for the moles next spring.

The lavender bush came from a cutting I got from a cousin who took her cutting from the garden of another cousin, for whom all we can favourably say is that he had a hand with lavender. Her cutting came away better than mine. Indeed the story of my lavender is more satisfactory than its performance.

Perhaps I should follow the example of Mackenzie, the Man of Feeling, who used to visit a neighbouring estate. "Decorating a place by inscription is scarcely know in this country, yet has the advantage that it prepares the mind for that pleasure which a beautiful situation should produce," he wrote. Should I write inscriptions to help out a peely-wally horticultural acquisition?

The Reverend Peter

Our nearest neighbour, who sits opposite us in the kirk, came up last Sunday with a distraught look in his eye to ask us to swap seats since, he said, "I can't bear looking any longer at the Reverend Peter eternally poised for oblique flight."

The Reverend Peter Ferries, who died in 1865, was minister in this parish for 37 years and a marble plaque to his memory is fixed to the wall directly behind our pew. The plaque is white marble, which is rather nice, but it is flanked by two small columns of polished granite regrettably resembling fatty sausage meat. The whole is secured to its mooring at that jaunty angle which so preyed on our friend's optic nerves.

* * *

The Rev. Peter (whom I find it impossible to consider dead) is the author of the article on Elginshire in the amended Statistical Account of Scotland which was published nearly 50 years after Sinclair's original Account. The Rev. Macdonell, who was later translated to another charge, did the parish piece on the earlier occasion, and it is when one compares the two one realizes how delightful a person the Rev. Peter is. Or is it that I think him so because I see the same things as he does and feel similarly about them?

He notes that it is all very well for Moray to boast about its extra days of sunshine, but in Braemoray which is the part we inhabit, far from having more than our share of sun, we have three weeks less. Like me he regrets the lateness of the crops but comforts himself with the longevity of the inhabitants.

He is conscious of the notable history of a countryside where the chief families were closely connected with the Scottish court, but is not so overwhelmed with the consequent feuds and stratagems as not to notice that, when Edward III relieved Lochindorb Castle in 1336, among those he rescued were the Countess of Atholl "and other ladies that were lovely." True, Wyntoun made the same observation but the Rev. Macdonell sternly omits any such softening touch of romance in his version.

The Rev. Peter knew my present home well. He knew the school now in ruins by the burn but which in his day was run "on her own adventure" by a lady who taught 30 little girls how to sew and spin. He must have sighed tolerantly over the inn which by the time I arrived had degenerated from a shebeen into a shed for honey frames. After a fool of a tup got himself shut in by mistake we took the shed away completely. The Rev. Peter would have been as regretful as relieved.

Like many who live in the Findhorn valley he fell under the enchantment of its birds. He spent hours watching the heronry down past Altyre. A few miles up the river at Dounduff is the seat of the last real Bishop of Moray, Colin Falconer, a cadet of the Falconers of Halkerton in Nairn, who were so skilled in the training of hawks and falcons in the seventeenth century.

Colin was a man of strong personal piety with the blessed gift of peace-making. No wonder when I see a heron rising majestically and watch its ancient enemy the falcon hailing a passing wind I taste the pleasure of immortal companionship.

Heather and Olives

Nothing brings out the flavour of anything so perfectly as the immediate juxtaposition of is opposite. That is why I found the autumn landscape of the Highlands so exciting when I came back to it after a stay in Florence, where even a spectacular thunderstorm followed by an earth tremor failed to alter the imperturbability of a sun that had been shining for months.

To eyes grown accustomed to grey olive groves and the terraced vines that drew miraculous sustenance from parched and fissured earth, the grass fields of Dalcross, lush and green after rain, seemed less the prospect of useful winter keep than lawns leading to a land where spring was ever young, and the sight of a peasant woman, gnarled and old as the olive trees she tended, unimaginable. Across the Firth the fat and fertile lands of the Black Isle rose and swooped. I thought of the vistas the Florentines are so anxious to show their visitors and wondered what they'd say if some extraordinary chance were to substitute the insistent loveliness of our far peaks for the gentle intimacies of their sunny countryside where the eye is at once caressed and cajoled.

How, I wondered, would the Forestry Commission, who have planted the neat inexorability of their conifers over moor and hill, feel if they suddenly woke up one morning to find themselves looking at a land where trees were planted for grateful shade and because their shape and situation flattered and adorned the nearer distance. Conversely how disconcerted would the Italians be if their ilexes and cypresses were vanished all, and instead, their air was filled with the hot sharp sweetness of that resin which intoxicates our upland atmosphere.

As a people we are obsessed with our own climate and we take if for granted that other nationalities must feel the same about it. Looking at the stooked fields between here and Inverness which wait the drying wind I remembered Rita the maid in the boarding house who sighed for Scotland where we have such comfortable houses "with coal fires, Madam." Outside the white sun blazed on every ancient palace, the Arno slid below its fabled bridges and in the courtyard of the Palazzo Vecchio 200 yards away a fountain played, showering beauty like the sacred river Clitumnus – and Rita yearned to draw her chair up to the leaping, cheery, dirty coal fire of a Scottish farm house on a dreich windswept moor.

I began to wonder if our tourist approach to our own country was all wrong. Should we scrap our scenic splendours and our pageantry and instead lure the sun-weary southerner with tales of fires and freshening rains and invigorating wind? But perhaps our contrasts are more apparent than real. One of the pleasantest memories I have is of the tall Irish nun in a guest house perched admist the Appenines. She scanned the horizon for a raincloud and

we spoke together of growing crops – what nurture they needed,
the hard work men had to harvest them.

Italy did not then seem all that different from home.

Watching for Winterers

I'm writing this while waiting for the second lot of wintering sheep to arrive. The first came in more than a week ago and are already at home on the hill, peacefully grazing and looking at danger spots they must avoid when winter floods the drains and peaty holes.

We hope to-day's contingent will prove as amiably co-operative. Anxiously I hang out of the scullery window watching for them, counting the minutes till they appear.

Normally we do not behave thus with visiting floats. All we do is yell at them to halt their lumbering career till we arrange the electric fence so that they can go over it without breaking the wire. But to-day it is different. The hydro engineers who have spent a vexatious 18 months erecting a line of pylons over the moor are now weaving a steel cradle over the main road. The scene of this tricky and arduous endeavour is just beyond our farm gate and since neither they nor we are eager for the sheep truck and its driver to get enmeshed in the heavy metal cables the job requires I am supposed to be around to give warning.

But if I lean overlong by the window sill it is not only because I am mesmerised at the sight of men at difficult and intricate work. October burns gold along the birch above the howe and all the pageant of a serenely unexpected autumn moves contentedly along the valley. The sky is illumined to that blue which lies within the flower of the harebell and down in the cup between hill and firth the Laich of Moray lies small and exquisite in the thin air. They have finished the harvest there and the tranquil fields lie fulfilled in the pellucid light of the fading year.

Nearer home the work still goes on. Because the season was late and cold there are many acres of oats still green as leeks. Tired of waiting for them the farmers who have potatoes have got to work lifting them. By the time the last pit is earthed up they hope their reluctant crops will be ready for the combine. The day of the stack is apparently over even here in the conservative hill.

The air is full of floating strands of gossamer and spiders hastily clamber along the trapezes they have slung between broom and juniper. Silly flies hardly hatched blunder into these silken lures and Dod comes looking for the tin of midge ointment he has not needed all our Scottish summer. If only the weather was always like this we sigh how could one bear to leave one's own country. And as if to give the lie to our foolish thoughts the first arrowing geese come jangling overhead, so high they are almost invisible.

Soon the horizon will be full of their swathes and tangles. They have no illusions about our weather and are already fleeing winter on our north bound shore. The stay-at-home robin sits on the old henhouse roof and sings his small pure song, its notes round and unearthly sweet. He is practising for the time when he will sing in snow and frost for our comfort and delight.

And here come the sheep. The engineers have already seen them and are doing helpful things with their tackle. I'll run out and do what is necessary with the electrical fence.

Shelter for Sale

Some years ago a benevolent county council told our parish that it was to be provided with a bus shelter.

While we appreciated the gesture, we could not help wondering who exactly was going to benefit from a structure just big enough to house a dozen pullets, serving a road nine-and-a-half miles long, where none of the intending bus travellers lives near the route.

Perhaps no one should have been blamed for advancing an argument in favour of his own immediate interest. Some said the hut should be placed where it would be convenient for the milk marketeers to leave their pint; others, who had children going to school by public transport, were all for the thing to be sited on the side of the road at which the scholars boarded the conveyance, and never heed whether this was on a slow bend or not. Still others commented severely on its suitability for leaving or retrieving laundry parcels. Could we guarantee that there would be no roof drip to sully the immaculacy of a newly ironed embroidered supper cloth?

Since the central council had intended the shelter to be used entirely to shield travellers from the blasts of Dava's icy mountains they paid no attention to the more flexible policies advanced by us; and indicated firmly that they expected the district councillors to make up the collective mind of the parish. So the minister and myself who shared this obnoxious duty stapped the gift into a hole in the dyke surrounding the kirk glebe.

* * *

If the situation lacked general convenience no one could deny it was well found in the matter of the romantic and picturesque. Sullen silence greeted our *fait accompli*, but eventually feeling subsided, and by the beginning of this year the populace were ceasing to speak pointedly about "the minister's (and my) sheddie."

I was just drawing a cautious breath of relief when the news broke that we were to be given another shelter. This time I plunged into an anxious huddle with those who were the most likely to have to deal with storm-stuck passengers. But I truly did not expect any sudden actual appearance of the thing.

We are so used to timeless paralysis in our county that we have come to treat direct action as savouring a little of bad taste and I was comfortably convinced that the second shelter would still be on the agenda when my term of office expires a year hence. I was disconcerted then when the phone rang to announce that the new shed was now *in situ*. I was rather led to believe that the horrid deed had taken place at midnight. It was in a place where no passenger had ever been known to get on the bus; in fact the only purpose it could possibly serve was one which my informant left to my lurid imaginings. Would I therefore tell the "Cooncil" to move it a quarter of a mile down the road – to the opposite side, gradient or bend notwithstanding, and finally I must arrange for the whole rick-ma-tick to be embedded in concrete so as to forestall acts of violence by the weather and the youthful inhabitants.

Since the last car-less family in the district has won a new car in a newspaper competition I feel little pressing need for any bus shelter. Would any more needy parish care to make an offer? Or does it prefer the wrath of the elements to impassioned public controversy?

Back to Antic Hay-Making

Everybody in the parish is behaving with the douce orthodoxy the fag-end of October demands. While this farmer has taken home the last of his peats, that other prepares to sell his shott lambs.

One neighbour borrows a pair of electric shears to prettify up his calves for one of the innumerable calf sales which lend drama to autumn in a cattle-rearing country; another jockeys for a place in the grain-drying queue, where he hopes to have the moisture content of his combine-harvested grain reduced to a manageable percentage.

* * *

All are in step with the season except the weather – and us. We are making hay. Our right-minded acquaintances stop us in the streets of Forres and speak to us in the over-affable tones they imagine suitable to people requiring psychiatric treatment. Then they pass on to consider what grassland farming can do to folk who were once sane.

When we went from conventional cropping to a pastoral policy we were prepared for the expensive business of getting grass established and for the techniques we must adopt for the proper management of the stuff once it was there.

What we were not prepared for was the effect of a preternaturally mild October co-operating with that spot of fertiliser we put on a field to give a useful back-end bite. Under our hypnotised gaze the grass roared out of the ground in great fountains and cataracts of green.

* * *

Now the paradox of grass is that in order to keep it you must cut it – it is a "harvest that grows the more with reaping." There are two schools of thought about how to cope with grass. You can graze it or you can mow it. Both have their place according to the season. But we thought that in our case it would be easier for all if we had the pasture grazed. So we shoved a cut of greedy eight-month-old stots into a liberal dollop and turned the electric fence on. The stots did nobly, but they could not hope to make their eating match the growth. We saw we must get the tangle of growth off; otherwise the pasture would suffocate. So the mower went in, and after it the hay turner.

But the weather which pushed the crop up is not the weather to dry it. Golden day drifts quietly into golden day. There is never a breath of wind to ruffle the holy calm. Only coveys of grouse packing for autumn disturb the silence in the October moor. We drowse under a honeyed opiate. And the hay drowses too. I expect we shall have to do what we once did with a much lighter growth a few Septembers ago, hang it on the fence to dry like washing. After that we'll rummle it somehow into bales, reflecting that though it will not make fancy feeding its real value is that it will be off the ground.

We are well aware that our haymaking reeks of the antic but what are we to do in a year when, against all precedent, the deer grass which was decently dead last month is now springing green from its roots and new scabious buds are resurrecting from summer's withered blooms and bursting into joyful purple along the flanks of sheltering hill?

Getting "All Glammed Up"

October got tired of behaving angelically and, throwing a sudden tantrum, went out banging the door so loudly that we are still deafened and have only sufficient energy left to be thankful we got our freak hay secure in front of the first snow shower.

We shoved the ultimate bale into the old milk house, a fittingly unorthodox store for an unorthodox crop. Since then winter has made no secret of its designs. It means to move directly to our back door via the snow-capped mountains lowering above the glitter of the firth.

Last week I was in Nairn, where the hotelkeepers, accepting the fact that the holiday season, as they understand it, is over, have decided to close the bigger hotels till next Easter. The Riviera of the North shrewdly believes in not drawing the tourists' attention to itself in its off season. Up in Grantown, however, they view things differently. The sight of the year's first snow throws the hoteliers into a tizzy of delighted excitement.

Last year when most of us were frozen to an icicle Grantown and the other resorts in Upper Spey were enjoying the first benefits of a ski-lift and taking a happy glance into the promised land where, at present, Switzerland is the chief occupying power. When Dr Beeching announced that there would be cheap fares for winter sporters the Cairngorms people felt that, if they had not quite won a Premium Bond, they had been given a well-deserved bonus.

Perhaps it is my middle age that takes the gloss off the sparkling vision of an opulent winter season at our door. The fact is that right now such a season is for the young, the not-so-rich, and the tough. It is true that the essentials for a romantic Christmas card do exist. There are superb mountains covered in snow, there is a lift and access, there is accommodation, and best of all there is a bright dry air which the cliché accurately says is "like champagne." But the set-up lacks the glamour that would make it the money-spinner the region desperately needs since the idea of the Swiss *kurtaxe* was turned down so uncompromisingly this summer.

And yet the kind of glamour needed is not too difficult to attain. To be "all glammed up," as my chic little hairdresser tells me, is mainly a matter of clothes, make-up, and hair-do.

When I was in Florence in September I went to the International Leather Fair. Besides being impressed with the appearance of the best shod, most immaculate men I ever saw, I was fascinated by a number of stands displaying items labelled *après ski*. The most memorable was a pair of ankle-length lamé boots, elegantly toed and heeled. If only the shops in Speyside selling husky Norwegian sweaters so adequately would add a line in Cinderella boots they'd be taking the first steps literally towards the kind of glamour that draws money.

Dedicated mountaineers and skiers may snort with righteous fury but it is unrealistic to underestimate the power and pleasure of the frivolous. If they had seen as I did a pretty Florentine flitting down the street wearing a Black Watch tartan skirt above a pair of glass-healed gold kid sandals they'd be happy to agree that the decorative washes out the incongruous, and if Florence can be glamorous no less can Grantown.

A Visitation
of Tinkers

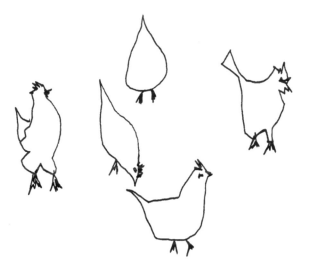

Away back in spring when there was the usual breenge of peat cutting in the village across the moor to the east of us, a tinker family came to spend an interval in time.

They found a heathery hollow by the river and there they erected what is known as a "clootie" house. A "clootie" house is a dwelling contrived from bits and pieces of cloth draped over withy hoops. Now in Moray we are against such feckless and unsettled ways. After all, we see what "clootie" houses can do to the approach to Inverness from the Forres side. They are the kind of thing that does nobody any good, either in the eyes of the sanitary authorities or the See Scotland First movement.

However, country folks have a side for "tinks"; and before exercising his legal duty the local bobby paid a cautious call on the district nurse – just to pass the time of day, and mention in the bygoing that she might care to see the newcomers and their two nice wee lassies. So nurse called.

Being much struck with the cleanliness of the family wash spread over a flowering thorn, she entered into uplifting chat with the mistress of the "clootie" house, who in her turn expressed such suitable sentiments with regard to the future of her children that Nurse, whose head is as hard as her heart is soft, went off to see the laird.

He, being heir to the tradition of paternal feudalism, set a house at the disposal of the gangrels and promised forby, that he'd speak to his peat cutters to give a job to Issac (that being the tinker's christian name). So Issac became a citizen in a brave new organizational world. He had an insurance card and a medical card; his children had child welfare cards; and if his wife had no cards at all that too was in order since married women are appendages in any family.

Issac proved both eident and deft at peat cutting and his wife continued her exemplary habits of the family wash, while the children grew in their own particular wild grace. Altogether the village found them a credit to itself. Bits and pieces of useful furniture found their way to the cottage, and if an element of pastoral tidiness remained lacking – well Rome was not built in a day, nor nomads rehabilitated in a six month.

Perhaps a winter as a member of the indoor bowls would help to settle Issac down, while the W.R.I. would teach his wife the graces of housekeeping. Summer drifted indeterminately into the back end and it was time for the peats to be carted home to shed and distillery stack. Issac worked as carefully as any at the tricky business of loading. Then when it was over he gave a party.

His guests were his own people, 17 of them. It was a lovely party, uproarious, alcoholic, and long. The guests enjoyed it so much they could not bear to leave and decided to spend what was left of the convivial hour in a henhouse which did not belong to Issac. Alas their cheery presence put the hens clean off the lay. Issac had to be spoken to firmly.

He received his rebuke in silence. Then when the moon was crescent he and his family took all the furniture, mute symbol of a respectable way of life, and threw it in the river. They took their "clootie" house from the midden and went before dawn. Whether the village regrets or envies them must be left to the imagination.

On the Pylon Trapeze

Since the beginning of the month we have been fascinated by the men working on the great cables stringing the pylons which march through the foot of our ground on their way from Beauly to Kintore.

We gaze upwards at their terrifying situation above the autumn world where beech and birch smoulder their late fire by burn and wood. Thirled as we are to the earth, we cannot help feeling awe and terror for those who make their living out of the dangerous air where the bright knife of the wind from the firth flickers through the vast ellipsing steel.

The dramatic locus of the pylon men's endeavours naturally focuses our immediate interest, but it would be wrong to think such interest either sudden or passing. For many years now the "hydro," as the North of Scotland Hydro Electric Board is familiarly known in these airts, has been an intimate part of our lives. It has touched us so integrally that we are surprised that the rest of Scotland should consider meekly swallowing the Mackenzie Report without question. We are outraged at the proposal to amalgamate our "hydro" with its southern brother. The southerners are equally astonished at our emotional reaction.

* * *

The fact is that for us the "hydro" does not provide light and power only. To it we owe many of our roads. We are in its debt for vastly improved communications over tracts of remote country and we are vividly aware of the contribution it has made over the years towards solving our unemployment problem. It is the most beneficent civil engineer we ever had or are likely to have. No wonder we are thrown into angry confusion when threatened with its metamorphosis into an impersonal undertaking.

The "hydro" has had to work hard for this affection and esteem. In the 'thirties when it was working in the Central Highlands the natives regarded it with the crafty xenophobia Highlanders conceal under their courtesy. Balfour and Beattie at that time were the chief engineers and suffered much under the natives' innate passion for banditry.

But Balfours were as adept at manipulating the Celt as at damming lochs and by presenting a smiling but inflexible front gradually came to be accepted on their own terms. When the joke about the garage that was built so completely from materials purloined from a scheme that all the owner had to pay for was a door catch from Woolies in Inverness, lost its freshness, the firm knew they had won.

Since those far-off days when angry Highlanders asked their member of Parliament whether he wished to see the shamrock oust the heather from the hills – a reference to the large amount of Irish labour then employed – the "hydro" has come a long way. Dams have been built, tunnels excavated, and work provided for men who otherwise would have long ago been lost to Scotland. We have, of course, light and power and we are grateful, but it is for its social benefits that we cherish the "hydro"! We have no intention of letting it go if we can help it.

The Best Laid Schemes

Smiler the cat is sitting on the window sill with her feet cuddled in the warm muff of her tail, gazing fixedly out at the blackbirds clustering round the dish of food in the garden.

It is easy enough to read the green and murderous profundity of her thoughts. If only the snow were not four inches thick; if only she could conquer her invincible loathing for getting her feet wet and cold, every blackbird would be a stretched and bloody corpse. So it would. Instead, what are they doing? Commuting confidently between their crumbs and the deep shelter of the dark wood.

Smiler opens her mouth in a white sabred grimace. A fat lot the blackbirds care. They eat their food and when it is finished they utter small melodious importunities for more.

The snow which is making life exasperating for Smiler, her lawful prey, and us, came a week ago. Some hours before its actual appearance, it filled the air with such menace that Dod went off to the hill to gather the sheep. We are not too pleased to have them in bye so early, but it is better than to have to go digging them out of snow drifts on treacherous and difficult terrain.

* * *

For once they came without objection, trotting along nimbly and neatly on their trim ballet dancers' toes. Now and again one would utter a plaintive bleat when she imagined she had lost her lifetime's friend. When they reached their new grazing across the burn by the hill in the lythe of the birch trees, they looked around suspiciously before signifying their approval. Soon they were settled peaceably and we breathed our relief.

I wish the cattle were as easy. Perhaps it is our fault for making up such a clever and complicated schedule for the three months between October and Christmas. We ought to have known we were due a dirty push. We have 16 cows with young calves at foot, and these we decided to send to the good grazing in the top field. For shelter from the searching winds, which are such an invigorating feature of our upland weather, there is the big L-shaped planting lying between here and the Knock.

At home the byres and folds were to house the feeding beasts, due for selling in the spring, and the nurse cows with double calves. Across the road the second steading, all neat and snod after yet another of these farm schemes for which my husband is such a sucker, was to cope with dry cows and weaned calves. These were to feed themselves out of the silage pit so conveniently placed for them. At night they could either hit the high spots in the alder thickets or lie at ease in the folds deeply bedded with sawdust.

Now the snow has come and looks like staying. The whole beautifully integrated plan lies in ruin with not one little bit intact. The first to move in for the kill were the cows with young calves who rushed home from their out-wintering to stand in a solid self-seeking mass at the steading gates. Bursting a catch they were soon all occupying stalls from which they either bellowed for their calves or for bales of hay – good hay and none of the stuff made last month, thankyew. All the rest of the beasts followed this chaotic suit except one solitary cow, Mrs Fletcher to name. She departed up the road towards Grantown. Of course she was soon retrieved but we feel she had something when she quitted us.

Serene Hearts in the Highlands

Those of us whose hearts are, as much literally as metaphorically, in the Highlands have had a sad shock to them this last week when Mr Cormack of Cook's Travel Agency observed in Inverness that far from living among scenes of splendour we were inhabiting a country which in certain ordinary circumstances was "the nearest thing to hell."

Actually he was gunning for the complacent hotelier who treated the tourist less as a guest than an easy way to make money. All the same we who live next door to what we hope will become a flourishing holiday centre were a trifle stunned. Perhaps our little towns strung out along the firth are not all that attractive to the tourist on a wet day or in the evening, when the natives retire to their own nice comfortable houses, where they can shut the door and put their feet up – the world forgetting by the world forgot.

Assailed by such misgivings I went to the nearest travel agencies to look for the local guide books about Forres and Elgin. Last week-end I enjoyed reading them, appreciating their lively letterpress and their superb photographs. In fact, I'm so pleased with them that I think I'll send them as Christmas cards to my exiled friends overseas. But are they meant for this purpose? Surely their *raison d'être* is to lure holidaymakers to the towns? In which case the booklets are hardly adequate.

One of the first requisites of any guide book is a map. Elgin produces a full-page affair at the back of her book while Forres manages three-quarters of a page – half a page of Morayshire and a quarter-page of other places, only two of which are positively identified – the Devil's Elbow and Balmoral.

The vague topographical set-up reminds me of the Aberdeen wifie who went for a holiday to Majorca. On her return a friend asked her where Majorca was. "Och, it's nae wey. Ye see, we flew." The compilers of both guide books probably do not imagine that their tourists will sightsee per helicopter but they do take it for granted that they will all possess cars. But even a car owner would welcome a clearly defined route to Lochindorb, the more so since there is a beautiful coloured picture of the place in both guide books.

I wish the people responsible for the brochures would go to town on maps. They can take an example from the Northern Irish people who have so entranced me with their reading of their own countryside that I can hardly wait to go to Lough Neagh where Fin Macoul, dressed in scarlet, is throwing the Isle of Man – an angry greeny brown – out of the cobalt waters while a purple pollan trout admires him.

Yet what does attract the foreigner to our shore? Once, under a hair-dryer in a Florentine shop, I read an article entitled "Why go to Scotland?" Its idea was to tell the young Italian barber that Scotland was a good place to go to become a prosperous hairdresser. The author enumerated the obvious things like mountain scenery and modern towns. But the real draw was Scottish women who – wait for it – "conduct their homes so serenely and competently that the incidence of coronary thrombosis in the country is less than anywhere else in Europe."

No Winter Yet

In the North-East country people count the onset of winter from the time the last sheaf is led from the stubble field to the cornyard. Not until that happens and the garnered acres lie empty to the visiting wind do we accept the season for what it is.

This makes for a certain magnanimity in our calendar if not in our anxieties; and we find ourselves craving for "winter" much as we yearn for spring at the beginning of our next farming year. "Ha'e ye gotten 'winter' yet?" we ask, meaning "Is hairst over with you?" And we congratulate or condole according to the answer.

In December, 1962, all of us have attained the desired season, though not without a heart-breaking struggle. Yet we are luckier than the folk living on farms more upland than our own. There, acres of corn still lie in the stook, while others, messed and bedraggled, wait the return of the combine that November snow interrupted.

For the farmer in such places harvest as such must be reckoned a dead loss. Somehow, though, he must get the stuff off the ground if only for the sake of the undersown grass, on which he depends for next year's pasture and hay.

All this lends a wry immediacy to the form which has just come in asking for next year's cropping particulars in marginal places. This form is really the old M.A.P. one with a new look. Instead of laying emphasis on cropping it aims at establishing some kind of ratio between crops and stock. Hitherto, marginal farms grew crops for cash – not so much because they liked it that way as because they were encouraged by cereal deficiency payments and the old M.A.P. Now, from the questions asked on the present schedule, it would appear that others besides Mr Parkinson have realized that "oats are an archaic cereal." The policy for the hill farm in the 1960s is growing winter keep.

Though you can winter-keep on barley, for the majority of us winter keep means the growing and conserving of grass. Already the agricultural boffins are lecturing local branches of the N.F.U. on how best to do this. The hardest thing they'll have to accomplish will be persuading dour conservative consciences that grass growing is not the sinfully lazy business they suppose.

We have been doing all grass for the last two years and the looks we get from neighbours deeply involved in straw, long and wet as tangle, as we pass on our road to market, show that they regard us on the slippery road to damnation rather than the easy gradient to Forres.

But there are headaches in grass farming too. Possibly the greatest is the establishing of a sward as suitable for grazing as conservation. Grass seed mixtures are as tricky to concoct as any cordon bleu recipe. The skilly farmer must manage to blend palatability with protein and both with his bank balance. Once the pasture is there you must never hesitate to give it refreshment when it looks dowie nor honourable burial when is seems that the most economical thing to do is to renew it.

I say nothing of the inconveniences waiting to be discovered when you come to feed the grass as silage or hay. We get our winter too and not without its own discontents.

A Ring Not Rosy

Smithfield is over with its ribbons and rewards; and upland farmers whose compelling interest is in stock look back at it with contradictory feelings of relief and apprehension.

They are relieved to find that the judge and they agree about their favourite Aberdeen-Angus being still black and comely, like the daughters of Jerusalem; they are apprehensive because they are now being adjured to market their produce with the same technical efficiency with which they rear them.

Most of us sell our beasts through the auction ring. We prefer this method to selling them at the farm gate where we have all at some time been stung by a pirate cattle dealer who insinuated that a deal which cut out carriage money for a float, commission for the auctioneer, and the waste of a day's good farming time all added up to reasons for giving him our beasts at throw-away prices.

Lively memories of such sharp practice make the sight of numbers of potential buyers elbowing one another at an auction ring very encouraging to the man who depends for his whole year's income on two or three calf sales at the end of the season.

In addition to providing an opportunity for seller and purchaser to transact business, the mart fulfils a useful social purpose. In an isolated community neighbours depend on meeting there to exchange their news and discuss their cattle and farming. At home they are immured by marginal hills and rocky acres which do not encourage a cheery get-together at the end of the out-of-doors day. Finally the mart provides that excitement which gives savour to lives lived often and for long amidst the dreichness of an upland winter.

But marts are not entirely meritorious – the ring not inevitably rosy. Some of their faults are due to human frailty but other shortcomings are thrust upon them by the farming traditions and economics which telescope calf sales into three months in the year.

Far too many calves thus have to look for far too few buyers. It is not much good urging better liaison between market and seller so as to even out pressure as long as the obvious way to farm in this climate is to arrange for calves to be born and reared during what passes for our Scottish summer.

All the same there ought to be some explanation for the peculiar adventures some of us have been experiencing this last season. A friend who is predominantly a sheep man took a cut of lambs to a Highland sale where he was bid a very low price. Thinking grimly of the cost of a return float with unsold beasts he let them go to a buyer who at the end of the sale sent the lambs back through the ring.

To our friend's chagrin the new seller was offered a price several shillings more than that which he had paid a few hours earlier. Five bob more per head on 100 lambs adds up to quite a lot of money – especially when you do not get it.

Another neighbour was luckier. He took his calves to market and had the same unlucrative bidding. As his place is nearer the market town the charge for the return float did not worry him as much as the parsimonious bid enraged him. He penned his beasts and when he saw trade reviving he took a chance and offered them again. His price improved by as much as £11 a head.

As in life, so in the ring, time may be a great healer; but as an article of efficient business method we beg leave to question its techniques.

A Blur of Snow

No one would believe that only three days ago we were howking out the snowplough with its home-made sledge in case we might need it to carry hay to the beasts sheltering in the wood below the cliff field.

Now with lorries making their secure way up the road to the moor it is easy to forget the anxiety and discomfort of that winter day which saw us shovelling snow from the entrance to the silage pit and scouring the hill in case an antrin wintering sheep was still there.

Snowstorms here are not all alike but vary according to the airt which gives them birth. Those from the south are the ones we dread most. They come down from the Cairngorms, grinning with a tight clear menace that matches the frost that surely will follow them and keep us for months in its grip; those from the west sweep in behind the cohorts of wind that force their way up every corrie and farm road that confronts them. They do not rest even after they reach the heart of the thickest woodlands but set up a headquarters there to last them out till spring.

* * *

After the snow from the west we send frantic messages to a neighbour who has a powered snowplough on his tractor. When he has dug the school bus out of its difficulties on an unclassified road he comes along and digs us out of our frustration too. Snow from the east and north is cold as death and suffocatingly soft. It fills the air with great blurred flakes that smother the daylight and lie inert and heavy on the ground. The quality of this snow makes it

139

difficult to move or shovel, but because it is so soggy with water it thaws quickly, and even though it makes a dirty fresh at least it spares us the discomforts of a long-drawn-out departure.

Our fall came from the north, which explains its blessed passing. When it began one morning just after the sun had opened an angry Cyclops eye over the hill we realized once more how accurate the Met. men at Kinloss are. They can smell a storm three weeks away and thus the countryside is pretty well alerted. Which is a good thing since this particular blur of snow gave us little warning but suddenly appeared in a huge bank out of the Laich. The small winter day gave up without a struggle and abandoned itself to the dark from which it had hardly advanced at all.

In such a fall, where the flakes are heavy with water, the air assumes a strange plangency. Noises, however far off, are relayed with neither echo nor distortion but with a plaintive clarity which speaks as much to the heart as to the ear. The diesel half a mile away sounding its horn as it enters a cutting and the burn still farther off leaving the peat hag by the flats both sound equally near, equally intimate. When a puff of air lifted the curtain of blurred snow the extinguished candelabra of the larch was momentarily visible.

We remembered last winter and were sunk in despondency but next day the thaw came and we breathed again – all except Stoat who donned his ermine to match the snow and now must cross the black road like a breath of embarrassed foam.

"The Manson" Fortune

In the year 1906 Donald Manson, a Scotsman who emigrated to New Zealand, died and left a will bequeathing his considerable fortune to a number of rural areas in Northern Scotland.

He directed that the money be used for the furtherance of education, and while several parishes benefit under the will the chief beneficiaries are Keiss, in Caithness, and my home parish of Edinkillie. "The Manson," as the trust is called familiarly, is in two parts. By far the greater part of its resources is for providing bursaries for "poor and promising" scholars of the districts; the lesser is for buying books – instructive books – for the enlightenment of the natives of the parish.

With the bursary part I am not deeply involved. This is a good thing since it lets me out of having to wrestle with provisions of a will drawn up by a testator who envisaged neither rural depopulation nor the modern educational system which is compelled to provide schooling for pupils, promising or not.

* * *

I am as grateful for this escape as I am delighted by my association with the book-buying. To one brought up in the tradition of no free text books and might scanty resources to draw on to make up the deficiency, the idea of having thirty quid to blow on books – albeit vicariously – is quite intoxicating. I almost forget that we have all this money because half our parish schools are dead and those which remain are but the centralised heirs of a once proud tradition.

At this time of year the relevant documents which will give the teachers the right to use the money have to be signed and as I fix my signature I feel that I am helping to repay a debt to school libraries which must be as old as my reading self. When we attended a country school the library there was donated by Messrs J. and P. Coats, of Paisley. Three glass-fronted bookcases filled with the staple classics lived in the draughty hall and we were allowed one volume per week. My choice was always finished long ere the time was up, and I used to moon pitifully before the locked cases hoping some magic would release another book for me. "Vanity Fair" and "Sketches by Boz" will be for ever associated in my mind with the smell of varnished panelling and a dog-eared aura of old chalk and older ink.

Not many school libraries had the luck to be underwritten by a Donald Manson, but it is a source of continual wonder that so many of them existed at all. I have an elegant white and gold "Mansfield Park" I acquired from a library in a tiny Highland school which neighboured the Spey in its upper reaches. The classroom wore a damp sub aqueous air which might have been appropriate for incipient fishing ghillies but was definitely bad for Jane Austen. So I rescued her, though some might have another word for the transaction. I have often wondered how she ever found her ladylike way into such harsh surroundings, but I never found out, any more than I discovered who thought the shelves at Harpisdale a proper place for Miss Burney's "Evelina."

In the last minutes of the general council of Aberdeen University there was enclosed a leaflet announcing the founding of a new society called the "Friends of Aberdeen University Library." How helpful if I could, in virtue of my position as executrix several times removed of Donald Manson's will, call him beyond Lethe and ask for his sanction to help a university in a way he obviously would understand.

Dates and Diaries

Since New Year I've been going round the house collecting last year's calendars and replacing them with their up-to-date successors. Farmers usually get a calendar from each merchant with whom they have dealings, and since these are legion, so are the calendars.

In the old days it did not take minutes to whip off the old year and hang up the new, since the firms used the same format annually, with only the dates to mark the difference. This year, however, the winds of change have been blowing as elsewhere, with the inconvenient result that the drawing pin by the window sill which supported last year's modest effort from Tractors, Ltd., must now be replaced with a stout hook to carry the splendour of this year's Lovely English Gardens, complete with yards of lush green silk cord.

Spare Parts, on the other hand, have gone all utility with one picture to every three months, a sobering comedown from the scenes of tropic splendour in 1962, which showed Spare Parts shouldering the white man's burden from Africa to Brunei, tight-lipped, but imperial to the last.

* * *

As well as sending useful reminders of their day-to-day existence, some firms draw even more attention to themselves by donating diaries. As I am partial to diaries I was delighted this year when I was given one all to myself by the tractor agency with whom we deal. As a rule I am left out of this free-gift distribution and have to rely on swiping one from Dod's surplus. Occasionally I must even go out and buy one. When this happens I have no choice but to take what is left over. This is not invariably suitable. Last year, for instance, I was landed with a cute little volume called the Lady's Diary, which is packed with fascinating information on how to behave on a week-end visit and make a bottle of sherry last out 16 glasses – neither of which circumstances seems particularly relevant to my daily life on an upland farm in the middle of Dava Moor.

Both the Lady's Diary and my new one have a page which, if properly filled with the owner's name, address, and details of one's next of kin, will allow the police to make contact with the correct people in case of emergency. I do hope they won't have to use this for me because facing this convenient knowledge is a page which says simply:- "Helical, bevel, worm, spur, spiral, and hypoid gears." I can see my mangled remains being sent to the nearest space research station.

Diaries are full of such encyclopaedic knowledge that they seem the only practical answer to the classic question of suitable reading for the desert island. If you want to be really choosy you must stipulate the kind of diary you want. My own choice would be The Shooter's Year Book – not that I have ever raised a gun against anything in my life, but who could resist a publication which enlivens every page with snippets like the following:- "In Cathay there is a valley frequented by partridges and quails for whose food Kublai Khan caused millet and other grain to be sown. He also directed a number of small buildings for their shelter, in consequence of which he always had abundant sport when he visited this country." I bet Coleridge did not know that.

Ice for Cooling Tempers

After a fortnight's capricious blizzard, when one day looked like a new "on ding" and the other promised a cold fresh, the weather gave up shilly-shallying and settled for a hard frost.

Now everything is on ice – and very beautiful. The firth backed by the soar and sweep of snow-covered mountains is blue as a gem, while the whole panorama wears an air of scintillating splendour. Our nearer world is just as brilliant. No twig amongst the haze that crowns the willow across the stream forgets its diamonds, no tiny nodule lacks the lovely intricacy of the frost. The robin's feather fallen by the bird table carries the crystal accolade of the Snow Queen's favour and the humble dairy window hangs up its flag of filigree against the moonlit winter world.

* * *

Man and beast enjoy the change to the dry bright air. The calves, who last week spent all the time hiding behind their mothers in the doubtful shelter of the old house, show off like the brave braggart fellows they are.

They swagger out from under the corrugated iron roofs valanced in half-slipped quilts of snow and make for the bale of straw which came in the contractor's baler when he arrived to deal with the hay away back in the summer. All the beasts are fed shaken-out hay bales to supplement their silage ration and it is wonderful how cleanly they lick up every wisp from the hard-packed snow. The straw is a new one on them. They smell it, throw it over their shoulders, and chew experimentally on it. Eventually they turn it into a Li-Lo on which they chew the cud while doing a spot of January sunbathing.

Out on the hill the wintering sheep are having a Spartan time. They were gathered in by before the storm and show but little gratitude for the human trouble taken. Three of them departed for a neighbour's wood and we had to go for them yesterday complete with tractor and trailer. Far from appreciating the care that took the heavy snowballs off their fleeces they acted as if they were about to be sacrificed in a bloody and Old Testament fashion. Nor did their behaviour improve once we got them home. They are now shut in and muttering curses against us.

* * *

Apart from the sheep, who are exasperating brutes at any time, the other animals are vastly improved in temper and behaviour. As long as the storm threatened and discomforted they were as irritable as could be. The calves pulled each other's hair and spoke back to their elders. The cows stole one another's food and miscalled the humans at the pitch of their voices. Bob the collie began a new feud to the death with Smiler the cat, who in turn was determined to maul the birds. This squabbling was most trying especially when, Bob having been kennelled and Smiler immured in the scullery, the blackbird was discovered giving the blue tit its kail through the reek while one robin threatened another.

Now that we are on ice our tempers have cooled wonderfully. We are gaily reasonable by day and cosily chatty by night.

A Change in the Menu

The snow-rutted streets of our little country towns are full of lumbering loads of hay and pungently smelling draff, all bound to supplement winter rations on outlying farms where the policy is centred on cattle.

Since it is no longer profitable to grow a big shift of turnips, trade in winter keep has grown immensely; and one need not be considered thriftless or extravagant if one buys one's winter requirements from sources which, because of bulk methods and modern techniques, can produce them more cheaply and conveniently than individual farmers could hope to do.

The cattle take quite kindly to the change in the traditional menus though some of them can be choosy about the draff, which is a by-product of the distilleries which surround us in upland Moray. But, on the whole, they are much easier to deal with than the sheep, which – incredible as it may seem to the townsman – have to be trained to eat hay.

The tale of the sheep who died of starvation beside a haystack is not apocryphal. Shepherds have their charges accustomed to the idea of hay before heavy snow comes to bury their natural food. Once, however, a sheep is encouraged to overcome its conservative palate it can develop a taste for all kinds of unlikely things. Silage, ivy, and windfall apples then become acceptable.

The creatures most affected by the altered winter-keep menus are the indigenous birds and beasts. Silage pits instead of oat stacks have forced the chaffinches from their ancient haunts in the cornyard to the thick planting surrounding the farm. There they hide till the hay bales are shaken out above the packed snow for the cattle; then they emerge in myriad flights to feed on the seeds thus dispersed on the lisping winter wind.

* * *

They never come to the household scraps placed in suitable corners by the door, but prefer to draw in their chair with the cows twice a day at the strictly scheduled times of breakfast and supper.

The birds who do not scorn my hospitality are robins, blackbirds, blue tits, and a single wagtail. He is the shyest of the lot; but that does not prevent him, when he thinks no human eye sees, from dancing in the air like a crisp bow of black and white taffeta ribbon.

Since we have neither corn nor kale we have neither pheasants nor grouse – a matter for some slight congratulation to our pocket if not to our sight, since we miss the adornment they lend to a grey winter landscape. The pheasants have a comforting tradition of handfeeding but the grouse are sparsely served in a countryside where croft after croft goes out of cultivation.

Owners of grouse moors may yet have to resort to feeding their birds. In that case they will have to deal firmly with the fox who will be only too delighted to stop by the feeding troughs to pick off his supper. A fox went past our door last night leaving his tracks insolently plain on the snow. Was he moved by hunger or braggadocio?

It was, however, plain starvation that drove the weasel in to the back door to gnaw the few raw potatoes lying in a box there. I hate weasels but I'd have felt the laws of hospitality shockingly blasphemed if Smiler the cat had caught him before he made his malevolent getaway.

Feet on the Ladder

Last week, between the blizzards, we thought it desirable to have all the wintering sheep penned and handled, an undertaking outwith our own labour resources. So we sent for the Twins, who are the answer to all such crucial moments on these hill farms where increasing rationalisation has made the permanent employee an expensive anachronism.

The Twins are the 18-year-old sons of a neighbouring farmer. According to immemorial tradition in these parts they are working on their father's place until an opportunity arises when, with their parents' help, they can be established in places of their own.

In the old days when a multiplicity of crofts straggled along the moor between here and Grantown there would have been little difficulty in finding a modest rung for their youthful energetic feet. But with these places steadily amalgamating into larger units it seems as if the Twins won't find it so easy to attain that bourne of agricultural beatitude – a place of one's own. In the meantime the rest of us are delighted to be able to call on them and hire their easy careless strength which lifts the most obstinately protesting sheep as if she were a kitten, and tosses bales of hay from barn and lorry with no more effort than if kindergarten bricks were involved.

The farming habit common here of settling one's young in farms of their own must drive the orthodox economist right up the wall. According to a well-known writer in an authoritative farming weekly, "unless Daddy can find £75,000 the chances of his son becoming anything larger than a smallholder are pretty slim." The Twins, mercifully, are not likely to lay aside their extrovert habit long enough to read this depressing intelligence.

Instead, blue-eyed and serene, they gaze contentedly at the fate that keeps them at home, where they get food, clothes, and insurance stamp in return for their work. Father receives the entire farm income, appreciating the fact that because it has not to be siphoned off into wages and overtime, he has a tidy sum to invest in whatever looks like paying dividends. Perhaps hill farm dividends are not extravagantly large, but if you have enough of them over a long enough period they accrue in a gratifying manner.

"Bairns and beasts," they say, "grow to money," and the proverb is no mere rustic jest. The longer you keep a beast the more you will get for it in the tail of the day; the longer a son serves on the parental acres the better and bigger a downsetting he is entitled to in the end. All this works out wonderfully well in practice, though there may be harsh moments when the young man rebels at what may appear to be having his wages forcibly saved.

Yet a place of one's own is worth waiting for. If Father still calls automatically for his son's help at a busy time, Son knows he can rely on borrowing from home the expensive farm machinery he cannot yet afford. I am not saying that some ladders may not cost every penny of £75,000 but they do come cheaper.

Crisis in the Cold

It was a measure of the isolation of these parts that when I came to this farm over 20 years ago one of the inducements offered in the advertisement to prospective tenants was the fact that the place was only three-and-a-half miles from a railway station.

The intervening years with the ubiquitous habit of the motor car have glossed over our solitude but we are still the same number of miles from the railway, which is, in the event, our real link with the conveniences of civilisation. Of course there are times in our lives when for practical purposes three miles could be 300 miles – a circumstance of which we were made uncomfortably aware the other day when a journey to the station took us up over the snow-bound moor to catch the train at Dava.

We could have taken the soft option and gone to Forres for the purpose, but we wanted news of a neighbour who lives in the Dava direction and who had to be carried out by sledge from his farm on the other side of Lochindorb to a waiting ambulance which shot off with him at two in the morning to the operating theatre in an Inverness hospital.

Neighbours, relatives, and the doctor had been involved in a nightmare expedition which made headlines in the North-East press. We knew that the road leading to his place was worse than bad, for we had watched a helicopter cruising round with loads of hay for him earlier in the week.

We were prepared, therefore, for a rugged excursion. Snowploughs had cleared a one-way track up over the moor, and the great drifts of snow they had thrown up gave the effect of a tunnel rather than a road. An access road leading to another farm broke the wall, and through the aperture we could see a tractor with its own power-driven plough at work on the crazy gradients and zig-zags down which the haulier would send his load of hay the moment he thought he could manage the journey.

But we had no time for the shouted conversation hill farmers use to communicate with one another. The road claimed all attention. The lengthening light of late January illuminated a lost world where the shrunken river lay frozen in its iced-up valley, its course decipherable solely to three storm-weary gulls who followed it from the air.

Behind rose the Knock of Braemoray, that frumpish little hill which attains dignity only when winter rounds its contours and emphasises the black geometry of the plantings at its base.

Thankfully we gained the station. A sheep farmer had dug out his own road there. On one of the huge snow blocks he'd excavated he'd written his name with a spruce branch for pen. In all the untenanted waste of winter the Highland surname thus incised in cold stood out with an encouraging bravura. We looked to see how clear our way was and watched the last dregs of storm drain from the pale cup of the sky. The world we looked on lay heedless of human crisis or emergency. We read the human name again before continuing the journey.

February Fashions on the Farm

Although we read the current descriptions of the modish fashion, our interest in it must remain, regrettably, academic. Because February shows every sign of following January's freezing footsteps, what we ask of our clothes is not that they should adorn us but keep us warm.

A fig for peplums and pleats, for linen and organza. We hug ourselves into the layers-deep embrace of anoraks and balaclavas, sweaters, and ski trousers, in which we have existed for the past seven weeks. One of the beneficial side effects of the prolonged winter sporting seasons of the past two years is the familiarisation of the indigenous inhabitants with the advantages of ski trousers for the female as well as the male sex.

So booted and anoraked, we are suitably clad for the weather. What we are not so well equipped for is ordinary housekeeping. Hampered by heavy outdoor clothes, we find simple processes like baking a cake and sweeping under the beds exasperating. Yet filling the coal scuttles and getting in the sticks calls for full protection.

* * *

So, as one cannot spend the short winter day continually putting on and off clothes, the solution seems to be to get rigged for the elements and then do all the outside jobs in one go. Thereafter shed down to decency and agility and refuse to put a foot over the threshold till tomorrow. Unhappily this simple plan never resolves the quandary of whether 'tis nobler to hang out the washing or peel the potatoes. To emphasise the human dilemma, an infuriated cow bawls from the steading to advise the world at large that her rights are being overlooked. She does not have to kick off her house slippers and struggle into thick stockings and gum boots every time she leaves the building. She does not need a scarf to protect her fibrositis from the north wind. All she has to do is stand with her friends in a warm, steamy bing, chewing the cud till the next meal of hay, silage, or draff.

Mantled in wool from their little black heads to their ballet dancers' toes the wintering sheep trip neatly past the frozen burn to the feeding troughs. Though their heavy fleeces sometimes collect huge snow balls they have the difficulties of coping with the bitter conditions pretty well solved even if they do smell a bit.

The creatures who are the real masters of the frozen situation are Stoat and Mountain Hare. They do not only change the cut of their coat but its colour as well. Silver-suited, they move gracefully through the silver scene. Smiler the cat thinks she has seen a ghost when she encounters them on her morning walk. Brave as a lion against the sober-habited weasel, she blenches at Stoat rearing his span-long ermine above the fallen larch stob.

I do not envy Stoat the immaculate cut of his clothes because he makes such a revolting living. I do not covet Hare her becoming fluff for she must go mad next month. But I do envy Squirrel in his grey, with nuts in his cupboard, wrapped in slumber and sables like a miniscule Russian prince, letting winter and the world slip to limbo outside the immediacy of his fur-lined dream.

Footsteps in the Snow

Since our unhappy notoriety 10 days past, when snowstorms cut us off from the outside world by road and rail though not by headline, the minimum essential services have been restored.

The result is that it is becoming increasingly popular among motorists living in the kindlier climate of the plain to drive up the moor to look at the spectacle of huge drifts piled up by the weather and battling snowploughs. They complete their vicarious adventure by peering down the chimneys of houses buried by the blizzard.

Naturally we who have to live here regard such ongoings as sinfully frivolous. We grunt our disapproval as the cars pass and turn our dour attention to calculating how long the silage will last if this weather keeps on repeating itself. Actually we are not without our own small if unspectacular diversions in the wintry aftermath.

There are two plantings here, separated from each other and from the arable land by an L-shaped pass. One leg of the L is trodden by our cattle and sheep but the other is used only in the summer. In the winter its track knows neither tractor nor human and because of this the wild creatures of the moor regard it as their private precinct.

* * *

In the unbroken snow which now lies deeply over its surface the hare, the fox, and the deer have left their tracks as plainly as print upon a page. Feeling like a pleasant cross between Agatha Christie and the Last of the Mohicans I set out to trace these footsteps in the fields of snow. Anyway it is more amusing than to try for sublimity amidst the sands of time.

Here, small and precise, are the neat footmarks of the old red fox; and there on the hillock to the right of the abandoned sawmill is where the hare crouched as he passed. Her two great hind feet are plainly visible, long ovals clearly cut at heel and toe with the intervening space fainter and muzzier. Her front paws are there too, much smaller of course but quite as definite. She must have leapt hugely when she abandoned her stance, for her traces are not decipherable again till past the ancient crow-planted Scotch fir.

There she crossed the path of a roe deer who was walking quietly, minding his own business. He had on new trim shoes, perhaps not so small as the ones the sheep wear but very elegant for all that. His tracks are easy to see and regular, so he must have been quite tranquil; otherwise there would have been some signs of those graceful leaps into terror which so often interrupt his life.

Hare and deer were on their way before Collie Dog came galumphing out of the wood where he found one silly sheep. There she is titupping along in front of him. He slipped on a frozen drift and righted himself after his powerful claws gave him the right purchase. He must have startled a pheasant as he scrambled, for the deep arrows of the bird's feet disappear just there. There is a rufflement in the snow where the strong wings scuffed the bright stuff and the bird became airborne. How deep and vehement such bird steps are compared with the delicate traceries the finches and blackbirds leave in the snow by the bowl of scraps at the back door.

Behind and below the walker the moor mottled with indecisive thaw stretches for mile upon anonymous mile.

The Yukon Trail

If you want to know what life in February means to the inhabitants of them thar hills read Dava for Yukon and you've got it.

True we lack the colourful trappings of pokes of gold dust, dancing girls, and saloons; only a frenzied imagination would see the prototype of Dan McGrew in the lorry drivers pursuing their endlessly snow-rutted journeys with supplies to the higher farms where the winter keep problem is a nightmare.

But we do have miles of frozen waste; we do have star-swept Arctic solitudes; and when the grocer's van does not make it we resort to the occasional rugged meal of beans and pork (tinned). While for lucky strikes, we are convinced that for the merchant and Laich farmer who have hay to sell, we must be the richest pay-load in any gold rush.

After 10 weeks of winter on the grand scale we begin to forget that Moray, not Alaska, is our native country. Which is a very good thing, since it has allowed us to come to amicable terms with our environment. Looking back at the beginning of the storms we wonder at how foolishly we fussed over what we now accept without demur.

Some people here go to work at villages on the other side of Grantown and use the train to get there. The timetable was convenient for the 15-mile journey and the hours of work fitted in well, too. Then Dava station went blocked. Schools of snowploughs became stranded in the narrow cuttings and the men who were sent with pick and shovel had to work so hard that they had to take off their jackets; and they hung them on the caps of the telephone polls.

Eventually the line was opened and a train or two ran till a spiteful blizzard wandering round saw signs of normal activity and promptly closed the place all over again. By this time the travellers have got so used to getting to work by looping the 40-mile loop via Inverness that nobody much cares whether Dava is open or not.

We took rather longer to get accustomed to our south mail arriving later and later. At one time it hit an all-time low by getting in two days late. Now it has settled for 24 hours behind schedule. For a while we found our newspapers from the south flat and unprofitable reading. Now we prefer them like that.

Somehow once the sensation value has been brushed off we recognise it for the meretricious thing it is, and read our papers as literature rather than news. It gives the reader a fine sense of lofty objectivity to read "The Glasgow Herald" centre page article on Mr Harold Wilson a couple of days after his elevation has been announced by radio. Our television shed its aerial last gale but one, thus insulating us still further from irrelevancy.

There are, however, some inescapable frustrations. The chief is our coal supply. We buy coal from one of our fertiliser merchants, which means by the ton rather than by the cwt. As by this time most folk in Forres are on a ration of a bag a week, we can hardly expect a large lorry to come charging up here with one lone bag.

On inquiry we found a coalman willing to supply us with paper bags of the stuff which we could cart ourselves neatly in the back of the car. So we changed the bags of calf cake which up to now we have been using for ballast and substituted the coals. What happens when we have to burn the ballast I shall doubtless discover.

Freed but not Thawed

The monster ploughs are continuing their daily journey from the Laich up to Grantown, intent, in their ponderous way, on keeping our road link to the South passable, if nothing else.

In these days of early spring, when the sun is bright and the wind blae, the moor alternately shines and shivers. We have never had a proper thaw, so that the worst of the drifts though long since scooped and shovelled aside have not disintegrated; but sculpted by the elements remain like buoys charting the course of the road as it climbs up Brae Moray and runs through the valley of the Dorback.

When the day is clear such banks and walls of snow melt into blinding incandescence, but when night returns with its blasting frost they freeze once more. Beneath the fitful shine of wildfire and distant stars they have the gaunt lustre of diamonds worn by a ghost. We shall be glad when they finally vanish, and sheep and grouse can resume their lawful occasions by the heathery verges.

While they remain they do not impede the traffic unduly, though every now and then a great block of ice unaccountably detaches itself from its parent berg to crash in front of the approaching lorry. The circumstance is more disconcerting than dangerous and the powerful wheels soon reduce the floe to slush.

Most vehicles experience no real difficulty, though the threshing mill still has to have special treatment. It sends an outrider ahead on a loud red tractor to announce its advent. Some minutes later it yaws horribly into sight looking and sounding like a seasick elephant; finally in the rear a demure little grey tractor beetles carefully along salvaging the casualties fallen from its predecessors.

We are thankful to be dug out and able to move around in comparative ease. But because we are not nearly thawed out our enthusiasm has its reservations. We think this a good moment to take a long appropriately cold look at the accidents which too often affect our lives here in winter. We observe our railway line closed for three weeks and learn with wry interest that this is the longest time it has remained blocked in nearly a hundred years.

* * *

We take a correspondingly poor view of the absence of any official shelter for travellers likely to be stuck on a notoriously stormy stretch of hill road. Here I have had men come shuddering in on a winter morning after having spent the night in the cabin of their frozen diesel lorry. Other houses facing directly on to the road itself have had stranded motorists night after night. Yet near and accessible there is a school and schoolhouse closed during one of the education authority's fits of centralisation.

We are surely not speaking out of turn when we suggest that such buildings would be serving a useful and humane purpose if they were turned into a haven for the blizzard-struck. The present idea is that they should be turned into a centre for secondary pupils who want to find adventure in the Cairngorms. We don't see much difference between that and a cosy caff for the long-distance lorry driver.

Calling the Roll for Springtime

The sun rises ever brighter and earlier above our upland world on which it shines all day, ardently thawing the great banks and wreaths of snow into the water which the moon at night can hardly wait to turn back into ice again.

All the scintillation of the day makes us feel we live at the heart of a gigantic candelabrum swung between the soar of the Cairngorms and gem of the firth – a situation which, though it may delight the eye of an artist, hardly encourages the heart of a farmer, haggard for some indication that we have not been transported for eternity to the Arctic Circle.

So far our only reassurance that spring may at last be on the way is the sight of the first of the new calves down at the steading across the road. When we feel the intransigence of winter too intolerable we go there of a morning to call the roll, greet the fresh arrivals, and compliment their mothers.

We arrange our calf crop in two lots; the first appears in September and the next comes along in spring. The division is useful because it not only allows us more flexibility in marketing but it also rationalises the winter keep. A cow with calf at foot needs much more food and general management than a cow whose calf is not yet born. Thus we do not have all the herd needing nourishment all at the same time during difficult winter months. Both sets of calves are equally profitable, but there is no doubt but that the spring calves are our favourites.

* * *

The spring calves this year are very grand, for they are enjoying the rehabilitated steading for which we got a Government grant. Outside the steading they have a self-feed silage pit well protected from the weather by an old stone dyke and an avenue of broom. The pit slopes off into a rocky headland overgrown with birch scrub and lichen and here they have arranged their nursery. The sun shines directly on it and the calves, sheltered by boulders and vegetation from the plaguing wind, are able to bask in its rays.

Before going to have their own breakfast the cows put in a lot of hard work on their offspring. Each calf is fed and then he must endure an arduous if affectionate toilet. He has his ears thoroughly cleaned down to their last crevice; then he must stand still to have his hair combed; finally the rest of him is subjected to a rasping polish under which he protests, saying he is not able to stand up to all this vigour.

Once the whole energetic process is over he thankfully puts himself to sleep in the very spot where the sun can caress most of him. There he lies cuddling his head on his arm. Sometimes in a very abandonment of wellbeing he lies stretched out, all his small body drinking in the life the sunshine pours so prodigally over him.

What pleasure then to count the thriving little creatures. What pleasure, too, to find a cow rejoicing over her latest born, to watch her great tongue massaging life into the rag wet body, to see him stagger to unpractised feet and nuzzle the warmth and love of his dam.

The Ups and Downs of Buying and Selling

One of the beneficial side-effects of farming's February Price Review is that it compels the industry to take an appraising look at itself annually. This year the scrutiny may well be longer and more penetrating than usual for Neddy has also recently come out with a report on the general health of agriculture.

We are discovered to be wonderfully robust; our wind and limbs are unimpaired when it comes to production and growth; but we have a tendency to hardening of the arteries when we come to market our wares. Not all our marketing suffers thus but our fat stock and market garden crops certainly do.

In a region like ours, where stock-rearing is the principal interest, this hardly makes headline news. For years we have been lamenting the deficiencies of our marketing system. We even have set days for our moaning. You should hear us on Tuesdays – after Inverness – and again on Fridays – after Elgin.

The fact is that marts have long ceased to be places where the only business done was in the buying and selling of cattle. They are, as well, centres of social contacts – perhaps the only ones easily available to members of an industry in which the conditions of work presuppose solitariness.

They are also the unofficial offices where many farmers transact most of their business. Here they can meet seed merchants and representatives of the big fertiliser firms. They can order next year's grass seed and sell last year's hay.

They pay their bills and sign cheques on the rough deal of the seats surrounding the ring. Some lazy fellows actually go to the clerks in the office and get them to fill in the relevant details on the cheque and then all they have to do is to sign same.

It takes a strong constitution and a hard head to do business like this, so perhaps it is no wonder that the elder farmers who thrive under such raucous conditions sneer at their heirs who would as lief buy a desk as a dung-loader and a filing system instead of a future in seed potatoes.

* * *

Actually, buying and selling in an agricultural community is a highly individual affair. Some North-East firms shrewdly send out travellers with a van-load of goods as likely to interest the farmer's wife as the farmer.

The customer who is looking simultaneously for the latest in bone daveys and an electric blanket finds this arrangement more than convenient. Similarly it is possible to purchase a dozen kitchen towels, a gallon of byre detergent and a polythene milk pail, all without going outside the farm gate.

Naturally farm folk would be reluctant to see this kind of merchandising vanish; but it must be confessed there is a need for some streamlining. Even the most hide-bound farmer today does not need three travellers for lime all in one morning. When he wants the stuff he is capable of reaching for the telephone and ordering the tonnage needed.

The same is true of all the things he buys in bulk, and firms could save themselves a deal of bother if they would copy the fuel-oil people who serve us and after each delivery leave a useful postcard ready for despatch when a refill is necessary.

Mild Days of March

Having finally decided to have done with winter the year, even in our unwilling uplands, has turned irrevocably to spring. When March came in on a mild and wooing air we were afraid to believe her and kept quoting the proverbial lions and lambs; we referred darkly to the storm which this time last year out-blizzarded all its predecessors.

Of course we had missed many of those signs by which in other years spring had advised us of her imminence. There was, for instance, no heather-burning. We saw none of those beacons on the hills of Ross across the firth which used to tell us that it was time we too kindled answering fires along our moors.

It is true we read with sad surprise of the havoc caused by muirburn in the West, but at that time we were suffocating under mountains of snow. When they melted we were in such a state of deliquescence that no one was daft enough to attempt to burn.

Now it is too late and the grouse who have survived a starving winter are free to nest in peace – that is if they can turn a deaf ear to the keepers and shepherds who are embarked on a final fox hunt ere lambing starts in a few weeks.

On Thursday last the hunt went through the plantation which thickens between us and the road. They made enough bellowing and bangs from what the Elizabethans called "a peal of ordnance" to warn every fox in the length and breadth of Brae Moray of their murderous intention and allow them to take appropriately evasive action.

We are also sadly lacking in the kind of vegetation which accompanies the front of March. There is never an inkling of rosy tassels for the larch nor catkins for the willow. But the birds have more faith than the humans and are back. Some, of course, we have had all winter and the blackbirds, robins, and thrushes are still about the door scorning our poor offerings in favour of dainties they find in the grass which now turns green under out-wintered implements.

But the real spring birds are here, by which we mean the plovers, the sea pyots, and the curlews. Green plovers – teuchats to many country folk – flap and mew from morn till after dusk when their loud hooting call makes them sound almost like owls.

Their brothers the golden plovers play and tumble above the moor making the winds sweet with their wild far-reaching cry. At night, when rain scuds along the sky searching for the new moon, sea pyots pipe their agitation. Only when the birds return does the lonely earth-bound mortal realise how much they have been missed. How companionable is the air once more when, like Caliban's isle, it is full of "sounds and sweet airs that give delight and hurt not."

For us inhabitants of a fortress sore besieged by winter, spring means more than just another season. It is the sudden easement from harsh intolerance, the granting of a freedom too intoxicating to be credible. We blink unbelievingly at the blessing in the air, the joy that invests the trees, the mountains, and the grass.

With William Wordsworth and his sister we enjoy the newborn world. Unlike them, though, we can't give even one day to idleness – not with all winter's enforced delay to catch up on.

Black Douglas, the Bull

Black Douglas is the name of the bull we sold a week last Friday. Douglas was his original name; but since no stock farmer in the north-east lowers himself to breed anything but blacks it seemed inevitable that Douglas should be prefaced with an adjective as apt in the annals of genetics as honourable in Scottish history.

Like many ordinary commercial calf producers, we regard the bull sales at Perth as more circus than serious, and when we need a bull, we mooch around among the neighbours looking at the class of calves their bulls leave. When we see a race of fat little black creatures with broad noses and broad behinds, we make cautious inquiry as to whether their owner is likely to sell the sire. If he is, we get down to the long, long bargaining.

* * *

This was how we came to own Black Douglas. He came from the bowery dales of Nairnshire – a small, plushy, waddling fellow with a benevolent eye and a penetratingly shrill voice. When he arrived our Scottish summer was in full flood and Douglas indicated that he preferred a home less exposed than the rain-soaked acres of moor adjacent to the steading here.

We took his wishes as orders and sent him across the road to the fields there which slope to the river. The Dorback has a funny habit of jumping its bed in flood and at the last deluge some years ago changed its course radically. It has divided into a number of rivulets which have in their turn created several wooded islets most suitable for a bull to take his somnolent ease after washing his feet in the soft brown water and terrifying all the trout and salmon. Black Douglas was delighted with the prospect, he plucked a marigold for his buttonhole, and summoned his faithful wives to admire him.

* * *

From time to time he would hear two other bulls belonging to neighbouring farms bawling fury at each other. At this he would bestir himself and climb the bank with more bellicosity than wind. Unfortunately, in war as in love, a third party is an embarrassment and poor Black Douglas as often as he tried to enter the lists, so often was he sent rumbling back down the hill. His screams of anger were piercing in their frustrate intensity, but they signified nothing. All he ever flattened was the dividing fence. Otherwise he led a blameless bullish life.

In the months that followed, his behaviour was impeccable and he attended to his stomach and his harem with assiduous impartiality. Then his first calves began to appear. Three cute little grigs whose sex we could hardly wait to ascertain. Alas, three girls all in a row. We were depressed, as heifer calves are not nearly so valuable as bull calves. We hinted darkly that if this state of things did not change for the masculine, Black Douglas, for all his amiability and fatness, was for the market. The next four calves were heifers. That made seven hard-running.

We entered Black Douglas for the weekly mart and sold him. We came home to find his first bull calf. Since then we have had five. Over the hill from Knockando, his new home, comes borne on the spring wind a high derisory laugh whose note we have good reason to recognise.

Change at Dava

Along with other inhabitants of that Ultima Thule which now looks like extending its Beeching boundaries over the whole of Scotland north of Aberdeen, we are contemplating our impending isolation with a wry foreboding which, nevertheless, accepts the economic facts of life in rural Scotland.

We have known for years that our own line could not pay. All of us could count on the fingers of one hand the number of times we went to the station to board a train. As for freight, our sole interest was when a consignment of seed tatties was despatched to the South, or a few bags of grass seed had to be collected in the spring.

Nor are we impressed by the argument that the train is essential to maintain communication in time of storm. We have a lively recollection of the three-week-long block on our Dava line last winter. We survived – a trifle inconvenienced, but not suffering actual hardship.

What depresses us about the closures is their social implications. In many outlying Highland parts the existence of the station gave significance to a wide, sparsely populated hinterland. The cluster of railway cottages meant a local habitation and a name for a lonely anonymous region.

The shop, the post office, and the handful of houses that gradually grew up round the nucleus stood for all the civilisation and company that the families of stalkers, sheep farmers, and crofters knew. Even in the era of the ubiquitous motor car this remains true of many places. The cost of buying and maintaining a car is impossible on the average agricultural wage packet.

The station offices with their high wooden stools, their burnished levers, their ticking instruments, and their smelly paraffin lamps were places where a whole community met. Leaning against the weighing machine, jockeying to occupy the one comfortable chair by the leaping old-fashioned fire, the countryman had the intoxicating illusion of sharing a wider world than that contained in his untenanted strath where all the company was the screaming peewit and the echoing wind.

The small bustle when an occasional train arrived stimulated him to such flights of conversation as he'd never dreamed of. In the to and fro of contact with the Big World, gossip ceased to be parochial and took on an oracular quality, illumined by shafts of wit and sagacity.

One of our most popular station masters was justly proud of his descent from the Waldensian Christians for whom Milton wrote that "magnificent collect in verse" :

Avenge, oh Lord, Thy slaughtered Saints,
Whose bones lie buried on the Alpine mountains cold.

The closing of our station hardly calls for martyrdom even were we the stuff of martyrs. But if our bones won't be scattered on the Dava mountains cold, a great deal of the essential savour of our life will expire among them.

April Holiday for the Farmer

When the wintering sheep go home in the first fortnight in April the marginal farmer who has been looking after them since November feels his load so miraculously lightened that he is encouraged to take a holiday; or as much of a break as the mounting pressure of other spring work will allow.

In our case we stood ourselves six hours' absence from the place and went off to view the countryside from east to west, from Dava up Speyside, across to Loch Laggan, through Lochaber, across the swing bridge at Laggan Locks, and home by the great lochs and Inverness.

It was not a very original tour, but in the spring sun and with a drying wind behind we had the chance to enjoy our countryside before the really heavy tourist traffic of the later season gets going. There is no time like spring for seeing the Highlands in comfort.

Perhaps it was the relief of having no longer to keep a lookout for sheep, either strayed or in difficulties; perhaps it was the firm conviction that we had seen the back of an unusually trying winter, but the land never looked better nor more prosperous. All the way from Grantown to Newtonmore the houses appeared to have freshly emerged from a thorough and affectionate spring-cleaning. Where were the picturesque but decaying crofter houses of yesteryear? We could not see a sign of them among the trim dwellings, all big windows and crackling with all the mod cons known to Ideal Homes.

If anyone could doubt the benefit of a growing tourist industry to a whole district, let him take a look at the confident bearing of Upper Speyside. Gone were those apologetic home-made signs advertising tourist facilities, vanished the muddy approaches, the cowering outhouses. Instead there were avenues and sun parlours, professionally erected signposts placed at convenient distances from the places they announced and spelled out in letters easily read by the speeding motorist. Everywhere there were cars with skis lashed to their roofs all making for the familiar sports centres which have become so much a part of the life of the countryside that the school children argue about the differing merits of the Austrian and Norwegian ski schools.

It was interesting, too, to see how trade follows the ski. There are ski shops all over the place and an Osprey shop at Aviemore. Bird-watching promises to be as popular as mountaineering or skiing. Will the coming status symbol from Nethy to Dalwhinnie be the field glasses worn round the neck instead of the alpenstock or the tweed hat stuck full of fishing flies?

We fled gaily over excellent roads, past castles old in story, through woods and by the side of lochs till we reached the fabled splendour of the west. There were daffodils blowing their trumpets all over Fort Augustus and "soft silken primroses fading timelessly" above Loch Ness. Was it because April had dazzled us that it looked as if, in spite of what we had been told, we are not living in a depressed area after all?

Where Do We Go From Here?

In our part of the Highland world we continue to be agitated by the fate of the railways we so seldom use; and as the weeks pass we talk more and more nonsense about them.

Perhaps we should blame the prospects of the pulp mill in Fort William for some of our wilder flights. It is so long since anything on a comparable industrial scale happened to the Highlands that it is no wonder our opinions should be tinged with the happy rainbows of Cloud Cuckoo Land. Perhaps that is why we are blinded by the percentage of afforestation in small Moray and cannot see it in perspective against the acres of commission land in larger counties.

No one would deny that it would be gratifying if the powers-that-are-to-be should suffer a similar myopia and leave the Forres-Grantown line open instead of closing it in favour of the Inverness, Slochd, Carrbridge route. One of my friends went further and suggested – albeit with tongue in cheek – that if all passengers were to travel free the cost could be offset by the saving on the salaries of booking clerk and ticket collector.

The railways have themselves to call to account for much of this, as anyone who has ever tried to buy the advertised cheap week-end fare from Forres to Aberdeen will agree. Had we but come an hour earlier – had we but come an hour later – but, alas, now is never the moment of economy. No wonder the bamboozled traveller reels out of the station to stagger on to the soothing, accommodating bus.

It is sad that such excursions into the frivolous should impinge all too immediately on the lives of ordinary men and women.

Here where we live, eight men's livelihoods are affected; which may not look many against the thousands also affected. But to them and to us it is the end of our economic way of life.

* * *

A scattered marginal farming community like ours depends for its existence on a supply of casual labour available at seasonal intervals. The railway cottages were the answers to our need.

From them came the women folk who make up the squads of tattie-lifters and tattie-dressers. Seed tatties are the mainstay of many farming incomes in the district, and experienced hands at the dresser are ever more important in a trade which depends for its existence on perfection, nothing less. One badly dressed seed consignment does not mean a bad mark against the grower only, but against the whole of Scottish seed.

The more we look at the prospect of emptied railway cottages the less we like it. Where shall we find the home helps for the sick and old in this isolated glen if there are no more willing helpers from the station? And who will clean the schools and light their furnaces? What about the helper so necessary for the school canteen? We know very well that the *raison d'être* of the railways is not to provide a pool of labour for rural social services. But we cannot help asking, "Where do we go from here?"

Offering Grass to Let

In spite of the protracted harshness of winter, the Laich of Moray lies green and smiling under the strong April winds, bearing witness once more to the recuperative capacity of its soil as well as the efficiency of modern arable mechanisation.

Seven hundred feet and more up the hill, we are hardly as advanced, but wonderful to tell, we are not so sure that we envy any more the favourable circumstances enjoyed by the Laich. Naturally we are uplifted as any one would be by the triumphant sight of springing oats, the tender ringletted braird of barley, the joyful flag of winter wheat.

* * *

But many of us have had a searing session with cereal costs matched against market returns and deficiency payments, and we are beginning to think that our brae-hung ground is not suitable for an operation which depends for profitability on conditions of soil and climate we cannot emulate.

Such considerations must be the reasons for the columns upon columns of advertisements in our local paper offering grass to let. We have come a long way from the time when marginal farms shyly offered moorland grazing for the store beasts belonging to farmers down the country. Now the well-bred advertisement keeps a deathly silence about hill keep and remarks instead on fields, well watered and well fenced.

The age of the grass is mentioned as is the weight of balanced fertiliser with which it has been dressed. Next year – who knows? – the analysis of the grass seed mixture will be added to the other inducements. Come 10 years more and all upland Moray will be one long green savannah – and not necessarily all for let.

Naturally we who gave up the unequal struggle with cereals some years ago are having great difficulty in maintaining our magnanimity and not saying "I told you so".

* * *

All our own parks have already had their spring tonic snifter at an appropriate moment between wind and shower. Now we are busy with the field next the hill which is due for direct grass reseeding. The process is long, laborious, and initially expensive. But when we incline to grumble we reflect on the drudgery in which we might otherwise have been involved had we not seen the error of our ways.

All the same, so contrary is our human nature, that when we see many of our neighbours still driven by ancient traditions, we feel odd farmer out. We could, too, find it in us to regret that turmoil of hopes and fears which are the inevitable accompaniment to every crop sown and tended by human agency.

Therefore we welcome the seagulls still spinning their silver springtime wheel above the upturned earth. It does not matter to them that this year we are using a new disc plough which we hope will be more tactful with the boulders left over from the last ice age. The furrows may not be the same shape but they are furrows just the same.

The old bonds are still intact; and the dear exasperating familiarity which makes each stone and rashy hollow an extension of ourselves is still as dear, still as exasperating.

4th May - 1963

Darling Buds
of May

To make room for "the darling buds of May," April bowed herself out on such a suave genuflection we could hardly believe her.

Under her warm showers and rainbows, the larches put on new green dresses and the birches give evidence of doing likewise by flinging their syrupy fragrance on every dewy wind. Daffodils fanfare amongst the grass; and shepherds, thankful that the lambing season is ending, hang their empty balsam bottles in the vet cupboard. No less grateful are their wives who see an early prospect of having their kitchens once more to themselves as the last bottle-fed lamb gets ready to stand on its own dancing four feet.

It spite of the merciless winter, the lambing season on our high moor has been wonderfully satisfactory. Of course those men who were frugal with extra rations for the ewes are savouring the bitterness of hindsight; but those who fed and be hanged to expense think the bulge of bills behind the clock worth every penny when they look proudly on big vigorous lambs nuzzling their well-fleeced mothers.

It is true that most of May with her unenviable reputation in Scotland's stormy calendar is still to come, but at the moment every prospect pleases and only tradition is vile.

* * *

We could practically forget the winter were it not for one thing – the absence of so many of the birds who usually enjoy the season with us. Living in a solitary place with few human encounters, one cannot help transferring one's interest and affection to those other circumstances which make up the countryman's habit.

The beasts of the field and the fowls of the air assume their own significance for him, and what scientists call "ecology" becomes the comforting familiarity of his daily life. A vanished tree, a burnt planting, an absent bird irk the accustomed usage of his mind and heart. This year we are sadly conscious of what the severity of the past storms has done to our neighbours the birds.

The larks have come out of it best and every morning is loud with their sweet gratitude. But there is only one pair of blackbirds to sound their trumpet voluntary to the morning and evening star, and one pair of thrushes to listen for worms on my tussocky lawn.

* * *

For the first time in over 20 years there does not seem to be a single wren though I had hopes they'd have found shelter in one of the two stout empty henhouses. The peesweeps who go to the coast in autumn seem to have suffered badly and the spring evenings lack the sweep and thresh of their angry wings above the questing collie's head. Curlews came off better and the hill is full of their piping melancholy.

Yesterday a gaggle of geese went over to the north in as ragged a formation as I ever saw. Perhaps they'll tell the pipits that spring has really come. We have no siskins nor yet yellow hammers. The willow warbler has taken over for the cuckoo whose absence at this time is so notable that it almost merits a new distinction among bird listeners – that of who was last to hear it first.

Almost Down the Drain

It was one of those rare spring days when the moor was lapped in sun, the wind came balmy from the west, and the sky kept reflecting its candour in the hundred lochs scattered in Dava.

The birds waxed lyrical in every holt and heath, and altogether we were inclined to take some of all that halcyon promise at its face value. In token of our cautious appreciation we resolved to send the cows with the September calves to the hill. They might not find much pasture but they could enjoy the view and stretch their legs. Too long they had been confined to a world bounded by fence and gate.

For once the herd was co-operative and bundled amiably up the narrow pass separating plantation from arable to the wide freedom of the moor. We were charmed and came home buoyant with confidence to administer a tablet to Little Bull, week-old offspring of Little Cow, who had complained earlier about incipient colic. Popping his medicine down this throat was no bother at all and we felt that with everything going our way even Pearl could be straightened out.

Pearl had taken her usual dislike to Queenie, her new-born calf, and had to be dealt with accordingly. There are mixed up parents and children in the animal as well as the human world and Pearl needs all of three days to take kindly to her calf. After that her behaviour is impeccable but till then she is liable to a depraved yearning to commit infanticide. All of which means a wearing time for humans as well as for Pearl and child.

So the day passed in all the occupational cares common to marginal stock-rearing farms. Now and again we'd take a look at our other cows cavorting on the hillside. Some of them were picnicking by the old crofts, others were investigating the rashy outgrowths by the network of the last hill drains. These drains are the fruit of many winter wastes of time when it is impossible to work the in-bye land. There are Government grants available for them, and there is as well the incentive that by keeping them in order the ground instead of being a bog will produce that lush natural grass that farmers like ourselves dream about.

Unfortunately practice and theory take a long time to catch up with one another. If we could count on even one scorcher of a summer to desiccate the bog through which the drain runs, all would be well. But such summers are scarce and the cutting remains a deepening cleft in the soggy gingerbread of the moor – and exasperation to man and a danger to beast, as poor Mona found when her fat little heifer inadvertently slid into one and remained wedged there as close as a banana to its skin.

Happily Mona is a wise creature and, instead of losing her head, shouted for help while she remained at the scene of the accident. Alternately she comforted her calf and yelled for the humans. Nor were we heedless of her predicament. With the help of a strong neighbour, a halter, and a judicious shove mother and child were reunited.

By this time clouds were again massing before the cold wind. Spring was over for the day and we took the cows home.

Nature Overtakes the Arrears

Looking down the Laich to where the flooding spring has brought prodigal new life we feel it incredible that the past winter ever existed. The first green of any year wears a vital quality but this year it is compulsive as well – as if Nature felt the season's arrears must be overtaken at any cost.

The birches have erupted from their buds, the willows burst their catkins into pollen, while the myriad wild flowers of our upland moor and wood have simultaneously exploded into blossom. The sun is twice as hot, the rain twice as wet as in a normal year; and both chase each other madly over the arching sky.

Birds and beasts affected by the energy of the time have begun to produce and rear families at top speed. Already wild ducklings, having mastered the art of freezing into immobility at the first hint of danger, are arrowing down the burn.

The sea pyot, who fancies her nest by the marsh marigolds still hidden from human eye, expects her two eggs to hatch at any moment. The late-come cuckoo calls from the hidden wood where she searches for a foster nest.

Down in the fields silky leverets crouch in their inadequate hide awaiting the return of the mother hare; while to our dismayed exasperation baby rabbits scutter their bob tails by the patch of scrub where the calves lie sunning themselves after their mothers have breakfasted and washed them for the day.

The rabbit continues to be a problem in districts where farming and sporting interests do not always coincide. It is useless for the Department to set up elaborate rabbit clearance schemes operated by grandly named Pest Officers when the resident gamekeepers do not wish to co-operate.

However, we shall have to cope on our own with the prolific rabbit. At least we know the drill, which is more than we do for the beastie a neighbour found attacking her hens one morning. Far from being discomfited at her appearance, or feeling any guilt about the two hens already slain, the creature turned on her, baring its vicious teeth the while. The consensus of parish opinion seems to be that the villain was a mink.

I do not know whether mink breed as ebulliently as rabbits, but, as the prospect of a mink coat seems unlikely, I prefer to think in terms of a moleskin waistcoat. We are engaged just now in an all-out war with the moles in the top field which has been reseeded at vast expense of money and effort. The moles are delighted with the results and keep throwing up fresh earthworks all over the place.

Wearing velvet coats and working indefatigably they give another and more sinister meaning to rising generations. And we are gunning – literally – for them.

Lonely Arcady

Nature Conservancy Week ends today and everyone hopes that its indefatigable host of participants will reap a deserved reward.

No one looks for anything as immediately massive as the National Trust, who deserve so well of our history, our beauty spots, and our monuments. No one imagines anything as imaginative as the bird watchers by Loch Garten who have done the incredible by turning the nesting ospreys into a tourist attraction with a conscience. But if the week does nothing more than emphasise the bond between town and country, it will have justified itself.

Actually a concern for the country and country things has been growing for some time in our predominantly urban population. The countryman has but to compare the pleasant manners of to-day's visiting townee with the boorishness of 10 years ago to appreciate the difference.

The gate-happy picnicker has almost disappeared and along with him the irresponsible fire lighter. In the next 10 years we hope motorists will have learned how to use litter bins in lay-bys; and by the same token we hope the appropriate authorities will get into the habit of having the bins regularly emptied.

The real triumph, of course, will be when the commercial lorry drivers return their empty milk bottles to the dairies instead of chucking them over the dyke into a park where the grass is greener and deeper.

But one must take care not to overdo friendship for Arcadia. I often wonder how much longer the war cry "loss of amenity" would be raised each time a new hydro-electric scheme is mooted were the ardent souls who shout it condemned to a long Scottish winter of paraffin lamps and no power points.

People living in the country, making their livelihood among its beauties and rigours, are entitled to some human consideration. Lacking it, they leave, and rural depopulation is the result. It is a mistake to equate desolation with peace.

Nevertheless some selfish country dwellers seem to like it that way. I once lived in a Highland glen owned by a deer-stalking laird whose feudal ideas embraced the surplus manse the congregation wanted to sell. Many respectable would-be owners applied to buy but the laird suspected they might turn out to be poachers. Not even the most frenzied imagination could glimpse such tendencies in the retired minister who was most anxious to secure the house. In the end the laird bought it himself to keep undesirables out.

The next time they have a Nature Conservancy Week they may have to add Man to the list of creatures in danger of disappearing from Arcady.

No Dark Satanic Mills

We do not know how much of stout Cortez's eagle eye the Minister of State, Lord Craigton, possesses, but he certainly gave our part of the world a searching scrutiny lately when he came to explore the activities and achievements of the local industries in Moray and Nairn together with the tourism of neighbouring Strathspey.

All the industries operate under their own non-grant-aided steam, and the Minister was impressed by the enterprise and self-reliance that keep them expanding into world markets.

We were gratified by these kind words, but surprised, too, since we have taken our economic activities for granted. However, we thanked Lord Craigton for his praise, while our hearts were sorry for the poor man condemned to dree his weird in the squalors of St Andrew's House or even the slums of London. To us all towns are places of dreadful night as well as pervading discomfort.

* * *

Which is understandable, since for our part we live one six months of the year associating with lawns shaded with "immemorial elms" while the other six are pleasurably expended zooming on skis amidst scenery as radiant as romantic. We admit that occasionally the weather can do the dirty on us, but on the whole it can be relied on to put a fair face on the Moray Firth.

We owe much to our climate and the aesthetic of a landscape notably lacking in those nineteenth-century symbols of wealth, mines and minerals. No dark Satanic mills cloud the serenity of our gentle horizons, and we are free to concentrate on developing family businesses which turn out comfortingly lush and expensive products like beautiful tweeds, delicious foods (both fresh and canned), and whiskies that sing psalms to discerning palates. We can do you crystal engraving in a studio waist-deep in flowers, and cedar chalets from a picturesque roadside yard. Do you want apples for your orchard or alpines for your rock garden? We have them both.

Nor do we neglect that staple of Scots tourism the legendry pile, the ancient keep – ghost and all. We have a ruined cathedral so intrinsically beautiful that its very dilapidations are a compact of loveliness.

* * *

Because we are a people anxious in ourselves for comfort we tailor our amenities towards such an end. That is why in our province you can eat such good food in such good hotels besides running around on roads to match the other excellences. It is true that nobody within the joint county of Moray and Nairn can quite explain exactly why the Nairnside roads should surpass those in Moray. Local superstition thinks it has something to do with the Earl of Cawdor, who is chairman of the joint county council and who has probably inherited the mystique from those witches who took up with Macbeth – thane of Cawdor in his day.

All this may sound complacent, but a side-effect of smugness is its ability to create that confidence so necessary to the encouragement of new enterprises. Perhaps others than the Minister may come to see us.

8th June - 1963

Some Noises Off

Once the great spring chorale begins we take its aerial melody for granted. We go unheeding abut our tasks while larks applaud the lift and blackbirds choir in copse and wood.

On the hill the plover calls the curlew; the dipper's brilliant song reflects the sparkling shallows of the river where he runs. The ear is so wooed by these Lydian airs that when an unexpected note occurs it brings with it the intrusion of shocked surprise. That is why yesterday on my way to the barn I was petrified on hearing the caricature of a cuckoo call.

We have a dozen or more cuckoos haunting our thickets who are so in love with their own call they go on repeating it all day. But what I heard was never sounded by any cuckoo – not even at the end of the season when the cry ends in a harsh gabble of laughter. I listened again and the next call came, less tentatively than before but still the same.

The syllables were correctly uttered but the pitch was far too high and the resonance blurred and cracked. A gush of warm amusement from the starlings nesting in the gullet or our forage harvester solved the puzzle. The same impudent little mimics had fooled me earlier in the week by pretending one of them was a hen who had just laid an egg.

Considering I have not had a hen about the place for two years I was considerably discomfited by their performance and vowed they deserved all the abuse hurled at them – though for a different reason – by the decent citizens of Glasgow.

* * *

Not all noises off, however, are made or counterfeited by the birds. We go every night before bedtime to count the summering cattle.

The other evening when the birches were clear against the westering sun, we found some cows and calves making ready to go to bed in the open-ended fold.

The end of May and the beginning of June can be treacherous here, for we are liable to suffer sudden unpredictable frosts that affect even out-wintered cattle badly. We stood looking at the beasts, admiring the glow of health that made them look like silky black plums, when all at once we were conscious of a regular hoarse breathing.

We had immediate visions of pneumonia and recollected with a sick feeling the year when we had four such cases on our hands – a fifth, a red and white heifer called Edna, had laryngitis, and the vet prescribed a mustard plaster for her throat. If you have ever fixed a mustard poultice on a calf you will know there are other ways of spending a frustrate hour.

We peered into the dark and the laboured pulsing continued. It was only when we had the wit to look above our heads that we realised the alarming noise was coming from the electric fence fixing situated in the rafters of the converted fold.

Art in Gardens

In common with every other rural county in Scotland during the summer months, we are in the throes of garden schemes – that imaginative charity which collects its funds from the small fees the public pays for having an afternoon's access to some famous private garden.

Our local paper is full of details of where, how, and when to visit; and, as ever, one is struck afresh by the number and accessibility of the great gardens of Moray and Nairn.

People have been making gardens here for centuries – ever since Robert Reid was Abbot of Kinloss from 1526 to 1540. Reid was a cultured and generous prelate who, since he was the first "to mortify" a sum of money towards "founding a college in Edinburgh for the education of youth," may justly be reckoned the founder of that university.

But his enlightened abilities were not confined to abstract sciences alone. He found compelling interest in practical things, one of these being gardening. In the course of his political missions to the Continent he met a former soldier who, having lost a leg in the wars, had expertly turned his sword into a grafting knife. Reid took him home to Kinloss to begin that wonderful collection of fruit trees which ultimately enriched Morayshire orchards by more than 100 varieties of apple and pear.

* * *

Since Reid's day Moray's gardeners have never ceased to embellish their craft. That is why the visitor can enjoy the lovely contrasts between the water-terraced flower gardens at Dallas and the ordered seemliness at Darnaway.

If so minded he can imagine monkish figures still culling simples from the herb garden at Windyhills which long ago provided apples for Mary Queen of Scots to eat at dinner. He can go over the bosky hill to Pluscarden Priory and see the old stone cavities where the predecessors of the present monks kept bees to gather honey from the flowers they grew in that rich serene place when they were not compiling the Liber Pluscardensis, one of our most valuable authorities on early Scottish history.

* * *

Nairnshire, too, can offer gardening pleasure. The interested can slip over the border into Coulmony by the Findhorn, where in 1738 Kilravock planted 2000 ash trees – "the first," his son tells us, "that were seen there in the memory of man."

Some 40 years later these rather regrettably inspired Mackenzie of Man to one of his more embarrassing sensibilities.

"How do your walks and plantations go?" he wrote to the then Kilravock. "If I were you I should be apt to plant stones merely to write inscriptions of them."

And he actually wrote verses to be placed on trees and stones to inspire visitors with appropriate sentiments when they viewed the scenes at Coulmony. The laird received them in silence, preferring to let his gardens speak for themselves.

Unready for Summer

It has been so long since we enjoyed an old-fashioned summer that when one does come our way we find ourselves unprepared for its immediate consequences and embarrassed by its repercussions on a farming timetable which was drawn up on the assumption that our temperature was to remain permanently slightly above freezing.

According to bitter experience we did our cultivations and slapped on our fertilizers so that, however indistinguishable from winter the upland summer might turn out, we would have some kind of grass crop. Now with the sun shining every day we are nearly drowned in lush growth.

"Meadow, grove and stream" if not apparelled in Wordsworthian light are certainly mantled in shimmering green. Flocks and herds enjoy such affluent grazing as we fear will unfit them for the leaner seasons which are the custom of our moorland climate here.

* * *

Naturally we find a country where sun and bright air combine in genial exhilaration very delightful. There is no more beautiful beginning to the day than to smell the old-fashioned rose-scented peonies shedding their too much loved petals on the dawn-coloured path. Nothing can exceed the visual pleasure of looking into the cup of the world brimming with sunlit afternoon.

If only we could sit at peace in a chair beneath the beech and give ourselves up to worshipping the season how beatific it would be. Alas that farming nature insists on rearing its ungrateful head; and the view that embraces the gentle undulation of the hill where grouse chicks are thus early strong on the wing, also takes in the park which we had intended for silage, but which now shouts to be made into hay. The cocksfoot grass is erupting from the ground and its head is already dark with the purple that will soon be seed.

Down in the Laich they have hauled in ton after ton of silage and their hay-making tackle is in operation. The big farms there have the acreage and other natural advantages which justify the purchase of expensive machinery. Here we depend more and more on contractors to help out with our rush times. Most contractors' timetables were drawn up away back in the spring when, because of the exceptional severity of the winter, everyone was certain that crops would be later instead of earlier than usual.

* * *

With the warm and favourable conditions we find out how wrong we all were. The result is that all our telephone wires are jammed with farmers frantically trying to make more up-to-date schedules, while our contractors have taken to skulking behind any convenient machinery in an attempt to elude the importunate.

In previous years we have been a little smug about our grazing management which depended on never turning the herd to the hill till they'd left a neatly cropped pasture behind. With all this riot of growth we've had to drive them out to the rough ground and its natural grasses before they'd finished eating the cultivated stuff. Now we'll be as untidy as anybody else.

Money Meeting

Every year the committee and the trustees who run the village hall have a mammoth get-together about policy, ways and means. Every year we emerge limply after three hours' discussion – so many Elizas on the ice-floes, barely escaping disaster and bankruptcy.

During our *sederunt* we cover most aspects of country economics in general and parish life in particular. The wider topics include the uncomfortable effect of the coming Beeching cut on our station and the accelerating depopulation consequent on the closure of local schools.

At the moment we are in the throes of a splenetic feud between two clubs which share a mutual interest.

The outsider, of course, must be cautious about the matter unless he has studied closely the genealogy which rules the politics of any rural community. If he does not recognize the roots and branches of family trees he will find himself thinking there is no logic at all in the quarrel.

False premises are bitterly pursued, he believes, to remorseless *non sequiturs*; while the blood of the martyrs is, if not spilt, anyway kept boiling. Letters are read, minutes consulted, telephone conversations repeated, and personal encounters detailed.

With the telling the heat of recrimination grows till it is a wonder the poor little wooden hall does not burst into flames. After all, it is insured. Perhaps a fire might be the purifying solution to everything and a new hall might rise like a phoenix with mod cons, to the gratitude and forgiveness of all bucolic hearts.

At which stage of romantic imagining the chairman rises with not a plan for a new hall but a draft for minimum necessary alterations to the present one, to a roof for the rural, the Sunday school, and the Christmas tree for the bairns.

The cost will be more than £1000 so will the ladies present not ask for stainless-steel sinks in the kitchen nor hot-water circulation for the wash-hand basins. At this all members register intense anxiety and utter Cassandra-like moans.

For two pins we all want to go home without consenting to spending £5 far less £1000. Then some exasperating voice says the public wants to know what has happened to all the money raised over the last three years at marquee dances held for the purpose of improving the hall facilities.

Where is now the money? The inference is obvious. We, the elected representatives of the community, have made whoopee with same. There is no alternative. On with the alterations.

Messing About
in Mist

For the past six days we have been messing about in a continuous Scotch mist whose only concession to change is to turn the taps full on and deliver a thundery downpour lasting for a full 20 minutes.

The effect is as depressing to the beasts as to the humans. Ewes and lambs loom out of the murk searching for one another and mourning the loss of family and friend. The lambs do not look as bad as their parents since their fleeces curl in the rain into tight little whorls arranged neatly down the middle of their backs.

The ewes, on the other hand, are wearing clothes badly needing a visit to the cleaners and the renovators. But as long as this mucky weather keeps welling out of the north-east we cannot clip, so they'll just have to go on catching their heels in the hems of their untidy skirts.

Nor are the cows less unhappy with the times. In a spasm of anxiety lest they came to grief in the deeper hill drains, we took them home to eat the bits and pieces of pasture round the steading. Instead of eating they made a dash for what shelter they could find.

In the mêlée a calf got knocked into a feeding trough from which it could not extricate itself and there, unbeknown to us, it remained all night. When found in the morning it was so stiff with cramp it had to be treated as an invalid and given frequent warm drinks and gruelly mashes.

The mother let us understand she held us responsible for the whole unfortunate affair. As she was bawling her head off at us the calf marker arrived, which meant that two dozen other calves had to be penned away from their indignant mothers. A shattering afternoon was endured by everyone.

* * *

In the end we were so furious with the cattle we shoved the whole jing bang up the hill road back to the rough grazing – drains and all. Every step they, and we, took squelched through that shallow fluid peat which in a wet period exposes the bony skeleton of hill places like this and emphasises their essential poverty.

In the fields the grass for silage looks like seaweed left over from the surge. Forage harvesters and carts stand around with forlorn drips at their noses remarking on our damp predicament and commenting on the poor prospects of next winter's keep. Hares plash around in the heavy swathes and the barn cats keep their quarters in case they get their feet wet.

But the gloom is not quite unrelieved. Last week the community held two nights of marquee dancing. The best-dressed couples wore gum boots and plastic macs while obliging tractors stood at the ready to help parked cars from difficult field conditions. The strains of "Petronella" and the "Flowers of Edinburgh" filtered across the drowning countryside with the plaintive melody of bells heard in a ballad.

We all thought the affair would end in debt but find delightedly there was instead a profit. Perhaps encouraged by this the sun will recollect it is now July and act accordingly.

13th July - 1963

Crowded Hours

In the old days when traditional harvesting of cereal crops was the habit here, our critical rush season was concentrated into the back-end of the year.

Now with the changing farming demands and techniques which emphasize the importance of grass and its management, we've had to jump the gun with the farming calendar and get our busy time over in late June and early July. Nothing will ever stop us hoping for perfect hay-making weather, but we do no really count on it and are happy enough to compromise with silage which does not demand all that much sun and drying wind, but gets by in anything short of continuous deluge.

When June gave up its first intention of bursting out all over, the countryside – which anyway had not believed in that much sunshine – took as one man to the forage harvester with its caravan of trailers. For the past few weeks, therefore, we have lived a life of grassy rush with hardly time to match the old records of how many stacks to the acre with how many loads to the hour.

Indeed, the men in the pit, spreading the heavy moist green stuff with graips, have not a moment to number the continuously couping hillocks. As well as demanding brute strength, the work demands considerable experience.

* * *

One has to know exactly how to disentangle the thick lumps of foraged grass so as to build it evenly and neatly into the ever-growing mound; one has also to find one's silage legs so as not to sink up to the knees in the still unconsolidated pile. Clouds of bloodthirsty midges attend the whole operation, and wise farmers' wives include tins of midge ointment in their weekly list of shopping.

Although the actual silage cutting is incessant while it lasts, it does not go on for the whole of every day. Each day's stint should have time to heat and bed down before the next lot comes home. In order to assist the packing and exclude the air as far as possible, farmers drive their tractors back and forth over the flat top of the mounting pile.

This looks, and is, a highly dangerous proceeding, as anyone who has glimpsed a tractor perched precariously on top of a straight 10ft drop of slowly setting silage will agree. But because the danger looks so dramatic, tractor drivers are more likely to founder to their axles than catapult over the abyss.

* * *

I am always glad when there is a halt to the merciless conveyor belt of foraging and driving, for I hope that then the wild creatures who make their homes in the tall secret grass will find time to escape the flailing harvester.

Much has been made of the "Silent Spring" book; but I wonder whether modern farm machinery may not have as much to do with the destruction of the patterns of bird and other wild life, as the indiscriminate use of chemical sprays.

Who now takes it for granted that the tractor ploughman will avoid the peewits' nests as did his horseman predecessor? Who now regards the baby partridges pathetically seeking safety in the dangerous grass so soon to be mashed through the Moloch machinery and into the attendant cart?

Changed Tune

Every interested townsman knows by this time that during and since the war Scottish marginal farmers have danced contentedly to the siren tune of the Marginal Aid Production Grant – known familiarly as M.A.P.

M.A.P. was that inspired agricultural measure which, since it promised to pay for the fertilisers, encouraged the poverty-stricken upland farmers to apply them. As a result the desert blossomed into cultivation and the most unlikely acres burgeoned into crop. But when peace came demand for our kind of crops waned, and for some time it has been a tricky business making out with things like cereals.

If it had not been for the continuance of M.A.P. many of us would ere this have been compelled to take a cold, cold look at our policies. But since the scheme was available we thought it better to agree with its demands and go on with the sacred rotational trinity of corn, roots, and grass. If corn was bad to harvest and worse to sell, there were compensating factors like cereal deficiency and plough-up grants to keep a teetering bank balance on the right side of the ledger.

Now after we have been duly warned, M.A.P. is ending. A new schedule is to replace it called Winter Keep Scheme. The fresh plan tacitly scraps the idea that upland Scotland is equipped either by natural fertility or climate for growing cereal crops. It recognises instead that we can produce cattle. So that we can go on to more and better beasts the Winter Keep Scheme promises us grants to help us to that end.

All farmers previously entitled to the M.A.P. have been sent neat little pamphlets explaining the change of plan. As a result, everywhere that farmers meet little groups of worried men can be seen doing communal homework — all of them getting different answers to the same sum.

The leaflet itself is a model of what such things should be. Its language is plain and precise; its examples concise and related to reality. Everyone who thinks he has been bad done-to is told how he may make his complaint. In fact, never has a revolution been introduced with such bland urbanity. There is to be no blood. Sweet reasonability is to take over.

Every farm in our valley is intimately affected by the new arrangement. From our windows the whole complicated pattern of our agriculture flows out sweetly before the eye. Here are the dark green blocks of oats, there the lighter — coloured lozenges of barley. The thin parallels of hoed turnips stretch out towards infinity and the maincrop potatoes reach the secret emerald of their shaws across the crowding acre.

As a portent of the future there are fields whose crop has already been foraged and packed into the silage pit. How long will it be before such fields make up all our mid-summer view? As our landscape is altered so shall our lives be. Old skill will vanish, new techniques evolve. Everything looks like being very efficient — and very painful.

Tutelary Deities

Tormentil:
Light, mixed and
deciduous woodland,
coniferous forests,
heaths, dry meadows
fens + swamps. Likes
a soil which is wet at
least part of the time.

There are two roads leading in to this farm. The one most people use is the shorter, which drives rough-shod up a brae before couping the traveller out at our back door in a flourish of granite chips and spent cinders.

One of our predecessors engineered this track, and sorely expensive legacy we have found it. When we are not engaged in repairing the ruts gouged out by summer floods we are excavating its course from the drifts of winter. All this is in sad contrast to the gentle behaviour of the original road which has been here ever since there was a farm. Without any brashness it takes its effacing way past the rising ground which divides us from the highway proper; then it vanishes into the green thought of the avenues formed by springing larch and spruce.

Sauntering by a little rivulet and past an old garden dyke it emerges at one side of the huge planting which continues up the hill to the moor beyond. Here and there it passes ancient gooseberry bushes which make a great show of leaf and none of fruit; and now and again it nods to wild raspberries and crab-apple trees.

In spring its verges are brilliant with the tapestry of all Morayshire's wild flowers. In their season speedwell and eyebright succeed tormentil and bedstraw. Wintergreen and purple orchis breathe their incense along its path, while songbirds hidden in the trees choir their happiness to the unmolested air. Roe deer and couching hare enjoy the sanctuary afforded by the inviolate forest where only pheasants flighting gorgeously in the undergrowth break the tranquillity. Here are the altars of quietude, the home invisible but palpable of a tutelary deity.

Country people everywhere have always acknowledged the essence of such places and as a token of their reverence have often given them names. When I lived in a cottage in the Highlands proper, the windows looked over into the flank of the Monadhliadhs. There on the grey mountainside hovered an eternal patch of sunshine and the people of the strath called the place it illumined "Johnnie's Garden." I never sought to inquire whether Johnnie was a real person or merely the affectionate name of a legendary presence. The appositeness of the appellation was enough.

There was, however, nothing legendary about the name given to a place which was the exact opposite of Johnnie's sunshine. Tirfogrein, "the place hid from the sun," was how Gaelic speakers described a farm in the Findhorn valley. Situated at the foot of a ravine, perpendicular cliffs shut out the light of the sun save for a few moments at midsummer. Yet the spirits of the place were propitious enough and saw to it that the barley grown there was the best in the district, while the whisky brewed from it was the finest in flavour. Alas that in the case of Trifogrein the Moray floods carried away most of its meadow land and with it the resident benevolences.

Benefits in New Neighbours

The other day a neatly overalled man came to our door to ask us whether we'd let him our empty farm cottage down the road. He was the very prototype of the intelligent, well-doing tradesman and would obviously make a desirable if unusual tenant.

He told us he worked in one of the neighbouring small towns; but, since he was a comparative newcomer, he was at the end of the housing queue. In the meantime he was living with his wife and three children in temporary accommodation.

With winter coming on some more suitable place was essential. We listened with sympathy but remarked that, unless he had a car, our house would be no use to him since there is an utter lack of public transport. But he pointed out his own small van down the road and assured us that he would have no trouble commuting.

We then said he had better ask his wife if she would care to live in the middle of a moor even though there were all mod cons in the house. And there the matter rests.

Time was when the letting of a tied house was not to be contemplated – especially if, as was the case with ours, a Government grant was involved in the renovation. But rapidly changing agricultural policies have reduced the labour force on the land so that an increasing number of good farm cottages are becoming vacant.

County councils faced with rising building pressures and costs are thankful for any help in their predicament and are willing to co-operate in smoothing out the old technical difficulties. The result is that a totally new type of inhabitant is slowly infiltrating into the depopulated countryside.

He is not the affluent middle-class week-ender; still less is he the shootin', fishin', and huntin' type. Instead he looks the sensible artisan who smokes an occasional pipe and grows roses in his leisure time. He runs a van instead of a car, knows his rights, and is likely to be impatient at our remaining feudal ideas. We look at him and wonder with a little wry amusement how he will take to this reluctant change into reverse gear. For long we have in the country been treated as bothersome poor relations who have had to be drilled and organised for the convenience of administration.

Our schools have been closed, our public transport menaced, and our kirks amalgamated. It looks as if soon Highland ministers will have to go on safari every Sunday to reach their parishioners. We know neither resident doctor nor nurse. We sometimes see a policeman driving past in a car.

* * *

What will our new neighbours make of us? If they come in sufficient numbers they may compel a restoration of some of the things that have been filched from us over the years, and by doing so force some salutary re-thinking on those higher-ups with marble palace complexes.

But since the counties of Scotland look like being centralised themselves in the foreseeable future it is doubtful if the new-style countryman will be able to make much difference to our lot. Still, it will be comforting to see agreeable houses sheltering admirable tenants.

The Walk and Winter Keep

The worry about the Winter Keep Scheme continues to agitate the upland farmers, who cannot believe that the crops they have grown from time immemorial are not going to be wanted any more. In bewildered fashion they keep on drawing up balance-sheets to send to their M.P.s in the hope that somehow they will convince the powers-that-be of the immensity of their error. All is saddened confusion which is not alleviated by saying that we must move with the economic times.

* * *

The other day we had an afternoon free between two cuts of silage and used our bonanza of leisure to go for a farm walk to the North of Scotland College of Agriculture farm at Clashnoir, 1000ft above sea level in the braes of fabled Glenlivet. As we fled up from Grantown into Banffshire the countryside had never looked more fertile nor more lovingly farmed.

The fields of oats and barley lipped the dyke tops in their abundance and every crop was eloquent of the passionate care that had gone into its growing. Looking at the cherished farms; the cattle, sleek as seals at ease on placid seas, one could appreciate the incredulous heartbreak of their owners on being told that all must be changed.

At the demonstration farm intending walkers had already clustered into little knots about the vehicles in the improvised car park. Each man clutched in his large brown hand a copy of the statistics relating to the place, and was dividing his attention between the figures and the lay-out of a new silage pit. There was a noticeable lack of that sunburnt geniality which characterises the majority of farmers' meetings. This was a day strictly for business, so when the gently authoritative voice of wisdom summoned us to listen we obeyed with unwonted alacrity.

In a way it was comforting to find that the enlightened had problems like our own and that a university degree did not exempt its holder from the rigours of cattle-rearing in the wastes of winter. Was it imagination, or did the high cheekbones and the cold shrewd eyes soften a little as Wisdom spoke of the difficulties of bedding beasts in the extreme cold of the past two inclement seasons?

* * *

We went from the experimental plots of cereals to the paddocks where the sheep were grazing. We had a look at the bull and a long, brooding rumination over cows and calves; we investigated the steading and its proposed reorganisation. It was the kind of farming with which we were familiar and the kind explanatory voice commenting on everything was reassuring.

Standing on the uneven cobbles of a fold due for rebuilding we were in home-like surroundings, and as we listened to the patient elucidation on how to farm the new way, we began to think the future might not be so terrifying after all. The art and tact of superlative teaching had never been better demonstrated.

The Lost Garden

Dandelion:
Fields, meadows, gardens,
roadsides, wasteland,
sparse woods; in fact,
almost anywhere. Likes
soil rich in nitrogen

Along with numerous other farmers whose places border the main road we are constantly annoyed by the damage done to our fences by those motorists who will take corners too quickly.

As a result they land in the middle of our fields with a trail of broken fence-posts and a tangle of wire in their wake to tell of the misadventure they do not bother to report. We have to clean up the mess and make our parks stock-proof again on our own.

The N.F.U. now wants the highway authorities to accept responsibility for these rents in hedges, barriers, and what have you. How successful the approach will be remains to be seen. But if anything does come of it the curving stone dyke that hides the overgrown garden of our farm cottage will be due for critical scrutiny since its presence hinders visibility.

The little garden is buried in long grass, but if you are prepared to explore you may find gooseberry and currant bushes quietly fruiting in the corner next the dyke. The currants have gone mostly to wood but when they do bear berries they are big and juicy as grapes. The gooseberries on the other hand seem to thrive on neglect for every thorny branch is heavy with sweet gold fruit. Thrushes and ourselves share and share about the secret honey-tasted harvest. When the gorged birds fly off to let their surfeit subside among the branches of an old ash the humans continue to eat.

* * *

It takes us half an hour more than the thrush to reach satiation. Then with goosegrass clinging to our garments and fingers pricked by the bushes we take our ease sitting on the grey wall held together with divots and interfacing stonecrop. Then it is pleasant to recall the people who in their day lived here and planted the garden.

Once there was an inn in this place where the hospitality was less decorous than the minister who wrote the statistical account of the parish thought seemly. These old boulders were its walls. When I knew them first they were bound with ivy to make a shed for the bee skeps belonging to the then tenant of the little farm. There was an old jam jar on a shelf which held a turkey's feather used for brushing the honey combs free from bees. One winter a wandering tup got himself shut in here by mistake and kept himself from starvation by eating the ivy. After that the tumble-down old place was rased to the ground to avoid any such repetition.

Poor Joe Albrecht, the farmhand who refused to return to East Germany, lived here during the time he worked for us. All through the long dusks of a Scottish summer he laboured, digging and trenching till he grew bigger vegetables than had ever been known in Moray. He left before he had time to tidy the honeysuckle or rationalise the scarlet rambler now half hidden by wild raspberries. Sunk in shelter, veiled in weeds, the lost garden pursues its gentle obstinate life. Repairing torn fences on our own seems a small price to pay for keeping it thus.

No Grousing About Grouse

One of the pleasant customs on this upland estate is that every year during the shooting season, the laird remembers his tenants with a present of a brace of grouse.

For the past decade, John, the keeper, has delivered them late in September and we suspected that some pretty nifty shooting had been necessary to bag birds which looked as if they were becoming non-existent on Brae Moray.

But this year, as near the Twelfth as makes no difference, John appeared all beaming smiles under his going and coming bonnet, bearing our grouse and asking had we ever seen them in better condition? We had not.

As we admired them, we indulged in comfortable gossip about the early nesting season when the first clutch of eggs was laid in the beginning of April. An equable spring followed to allow the chicks to grow evenly without any of the setbacks which might have proved dangerous in the cold sunless summer. While we chatted we were watching a covey of 11 birds feeding tranquilly in the grass park into which the fattening lambs are to be moved this week.

Eleven is a generous number but 15 is not uncommon in this vintage year. Yet the last time our hill was considered worth shooting over was six years ago and then the bag was a measly four birds. Up in Badenoch – if you are to believe them – there was none of our catastrophic decline; the season maintained its customary bags and its panache.

We are gratified as surprised by the sudden increase in the grouse population. By all the rules hitherto held sacred they should be extinct. The hill was burned savagely for a number of years; it was drained and rampaged over by our cows and sheep; and as a final insult, for four years we have not grown a grain of that corn which used to be considered necessary autumn feeding for a healthy stock of birds.

We have had two appalling winters and according to a neighbour who ought to know, tick is on the increase. But the grouse have multiplied as have the mountain hares. Because we believe that conditions that are favourable for these creatures are also favourable for sheep we are delighted.

But it seems ludicrous that so much should remain mystery and conjecture in a business involving so much hard cash. When a week's sport on a moor can cost upwards of £300 for a single gun, one would have imagined that some homework on the grouse that lays these golden eggs is overdue.

Given the scientific facilities one could have no more entrancing occupation than finding out about the flora and fauna of a Highland hill. The only other competitor in the field would be the fox who has already moved in to survey the terrain and startle our cows into bellows at six a.m. of a wet August morn.

A Look at the Library

Just the other day Elgin library opened a charming new reference room on the ground floor of the old lodge which houses the town and county branches of the service.

We are extraordinarily lucky in our part of the world in that the local libraries at Elgin, Forres, and Nairn are situated in the ex-mansions of county families. The grounds surrounding them have been acquired with the buildings, and, since gardening here enjoys a venerable expertise, the result is unique and enviable.

Perhaps we do not have the great book collections of national libraries, but readers are provided with those facilities which help to narrow the gap between the artistic and the mundane. Reading "A Midsummer-Night's Dream" in the garden lying outside the library door is to know that the lovely stuff between the covers is a part of life – not an escape from it – a thought to be commended to Walter Mittys and Billy Liars.

Comparisons can be dangerous as well as odious, and he would be a wise man who kept quiet on his preference between the bloom of ecclesiastical urbanity emanating from the ruined cathedral, manses, and colleges which margin Elgin's park and the velvet intimacy of lawn and flower that gives Grant Park in Forres its beautiful individuality; while who would be foolish enough to rival either with the ingenious cunning that gives spontaneity to the paths leading from Nairn's library to the shore?

What cannot be denied, of course, is that in the matter of actual building Elgin enjoys V.I.P. treatment. Grant Lodge, which is the place's baptismal name, lives in an odour of paint and rolls of wallpaper; so much so that one suspects that the spirit that was responsible for the cathedral and its precincts is still potent and at large.

A trusting committee orders a simple lick of paint, and the painter, almost it seems without his volition, finds himself compelled to embark on something far more ambitious than the terms of his covenant. "He takes an interest," said the librarian, casting a proud if surprised eye on the delicately picked out plaster decoration of the roof and the exquisite detail by the great windows stretching from floor to ceiling and looking out on dark red begonias and seats where old men take their autumn ease beneath trees still rich in foliage.

In the new "ref." the bronze head of Ramsay MacDonald bends a benevolent gaze on the bookshelves lining the walls. In one of them there is a collection of freshly bound local books and the inquirer may equally consult Lachlan Shaw, the most eminent historian of Moray; and – if his Latin be still usable – Florentius Volusenus on Tranquillity of Mind. In such surroundings and amid such traditions it would seem an impertinence not to brush up that ancient tongue.

Scooping the Pool

Compulsive week-end reading for the average countryman is neither the Sunday newspaper however titillated with sensationalism, nor the classic however pre-digested by TV and radio.

What he absorbs with passionate concentration are the advertisement columns of his local weekly newspaper, for in those (to the outsider unlikely looking) wants, sales, and farms to rent, he is reading his native economic history as well as glimpsing the prospects for his own material advancement.

Naturally, the items detailed have varying appeals at different times of the year. No one in his senses looks for a combine harvester in the middle of February; likewise no one is daft enough to announce that he has beasts to sell when the scarcity of keep is an uncomfortable fact of life in the neighbourhood. But there are some announcements that have perennial fascination. These are the ones about farms to let or for sale; the "to lets" have the edge on the "for sales".

For many years when farms in upland districts came on the market it was the habit to mention among other inducements the Government grants for which the place was eligible. Of these the chief was M.A.P. Now that this scheme is going amid such general wailing there has had to be a change in the wording of the advertisements. Amalgamation of holdings seems the up-to-date answer to what makes a desirable unit. The estate owner who wants a big rent must offer a big acreage, and if he can let his marginal farms by the brace so much the better.

The opportunity of such multiple renting does not often occur since neighbouring leases do not run simultaneously and death, the not seldom terminator of such contracts, ignores the convenient terms of Martinmas and Whitsunday. The prospects for scooping as it were the whole of the agricultural potential of a farming district are neither bright nor immediate. Nevertheless amalgamation has been going on gradually and with the new look in marginal farming its pace must accelerate. For the young man stuck by inheritance on a family farm too small by today's standards to be viable, the position is frustrating.

He can, of course, follow the example of one of our young friends who has taken a job part time with a very well-known firm of seeds merchants who can use his friendly manner and practical experience to their own and his advantage. Travelling round the countryside he hopes to find as well as customers a parish full of ageing farmers whom he can persuade to retire.

It does not follow that such a mass departure will necessarily allow him to scoop that particular pool. My own guess is that ultimately he'll find a full-term job with his firm the cheerier prospect.

The Last Line

Centenaries are useful moments in time for burnishing up one's sense of history. Along with L.V. Beharrell (in last week's "Glasgow Herald") we in our remote upland district are contemplating with mixed feelings the centenary of our stretch of what used to be known as the Highland Railway. Alas that its century should so nearly coincide with its execution under the Beeching axe!

* * *

We acknowledge sadly that as a paying proposition in British Railways we have not a wheel to turn, a diesel horn to sound. We never travel by rail. We have not even the excuse that come wind, come winter the train always gets through, since (although Mr Beharrell was too tactful to say so) last winter it took three solid weeks to cut through the drifts at Dava and resume communication with the South.

All the same, in this centenary week we lament the passing of our railroad and that the more because we have no cogent or practical reasons for keeping it. The feeling of being abandoned by civilisation is hardly an excuse that cuts much ice today.

An old friend who spent the early part of his life as a clerk on the Highland line was describing to me the other day how it felt to be part of an undertaking which did so much for the Highlands and their people. Along with the minister and the school master, the stationmaster and his clerk were the other literate influences in the glens.

Their days were spent not so much on railway work proper as in filling in forms, writing letters, and generally advising their clients-cum-passengers.

Unlike the other members of the quorum they were completely secular, and there were no undertones of ecclesiastical jurisdiction in the cheerful office where paraffin lamps shone on the polished brasses of signal levers and splendidly prodigal fires gave back reflections on high stools and the ponderous engravings of vast caverns of safes. There was an atmosphere of adventurous good fellowship. Travel was more than prosaic going from one place to another. It was an odyssey and Ulysses was a railway guard.

But clerk and stationmaster with all their impressive familiarity with the written word were also symbols of horizons wider than the glen and shores farther than the tempestuous loch. The station stood in all its purposeful commotion for a kindlier and easier way of life than men had dreamed. When the railway came from Forres past Croy the then Earl of Cawdor gave every man on his estate a whole holiday to go to see the *ferly* of the new railway and the engine.

It was the first holiday apart from Sunday and New Year they had ever enjoyed and it made such an impact on them that their grandchildren recall it.

How sad then that the use we have made of our railway was to board its trains and take tickets marked "No Return".

Scholar Gypsy, German

We saw him on the east side of Forres when we were speeding to the mart in Elgin and exclaiming on the abominable smell three Cheviot lambs had left in the back of the estate car.

As a rule we do not pick up hitchers because we are habitually loaded with other things; of the aforementioned lambs. But this lad with a blonde crew cut wore an expression of such modest pathos we could not resist his inquiring thumb.

He scrambled aboard asking if we were going to Aberdeen, so we said not quite so far but would Elgin do? He smiled happily, gazing in the stupefied way strangers to Moray do when they see her all dressed up for autumn and behaving with an elegant decorum that matches the sleekly shining sea and the golden harvest fields.

* * *

Our passenger was a German student from Hamburg over in this country to learn English. He had been two months at a special language school in London; and if his idiomatic proficiency was anything to go by, he'd made admirable use of his lessons. I could not forbear admiring comment, to which he replied becomingly that he'd studied English at school and therefore he was not starting from scratch. In order to pay for his classes he'd taken a job as a dish washer in a restaurant, which was very convenient, since in addition to paying him his bosses also fed him. This was no small consideration, for his room cost him £3 a week plus shillings for gas and electricity; no bathroom, no. But why speak about London when he was treating himself to three days with autumn in Scotland?

We fled past Alves where pink dahlias pretended they were soup plates and the flat rich Laich moved ecstatic shoulders under the clear hot sun. Our scholar gypsy said as we passed the little country school he was going to be a teacher of Latin and Sport. No, he did not think it a surprising combination, *mens sana* you know. I said I hoped he would not get his lines crossed and issue commands in Latin to his aspiring athletes, though we agreed that a ringing Virgilian hexameter took a lot of beating in the way of stirring the imagination and muscle. Yes, he sighed, Latin could be a bit stiff especially the grammar. But then its literature was mercifully complete whereas in modern languages writers went on writing and the student had to go on reading them.

By now we were into the traffic confusion which turns mart day into an agricultural nightmare and we left our scholar in a place convenient for a further lift from the friendly lorry drivers he had found as impressive in their way as our scenery.

Anyone for the Hairst?

Donnie, our neighbour and local agricultural contractor, went orbiting up the brae this morning aboard his huge sulphur-yellow combine, en route to deal with those corn fields that skirt the Cairngorms.

How many more seasons there will continue to be such crops in these hill places is a moot point but till the winter keep scheme is fully established I expect cereals will still be grown if for nothing more than their bedding value.

The nine grouse who have apparently moved into domesticity in the grass park fronting our kitchen windows hardly batted a scarlet eyebrow at the sound of Donny's progress. The starlings, however, still find the noise of the big engine novel enough to keep them practising it so they may add a new mimicry to a repertoire which includes a hen rejoicing over a new egg and a burn flowing over a boulder in its shallows.

Down in the Laich the corn fields are for the most part bare and baled though some of those worst affected by an unseasonable summer still await attention. Behind the farm buildings rise the silver corrugations that make up part of the grain-drying plant many farmers have installed.

* * *

No wonder the local paper carried one contractor's small, sad announcement that he was giving up the threshing mill part of his business. The new pattern of farming is emerging clear and determined for all to see – arable in the plain; pastoral in the hill. And both are being pursued energetically in the light of to-morrow's agricultural know-how.

Not all of us find ourselves happy or at ease in the modern set-up and older farmers look back with longing to that other shore where men and not machines toiled in company among the fields. As if to encourage such traditionalists the weather has decided to behave according to story book autumnal convention. Calm skies bless the adoring earth; hedgerows are triumphant with red rowans and wild rose haws; birches utter their first gold notes and day is all fulfilment.

Come night the wind rises. We hear it first stirring in the fir plantations. By the time the moon has slipped into her first quarter it is flowing freely through the beech and gean preparatory to taking off to fill the great sails of night which are to drive the ship of the world across the sky, past the Archer, past the Plough, past the Pleiades, and on to quiet harbourage at dawn.

After such favouring nights the most matter-of-fact countryman has a pang for the glorious reeshling past when corn stooks thronged the bindered fields and harvest carts rumbled all day into the stack yard. But there is no time for delay, still less for regrets. Seize the phone and ask the salesman who used to supply binder tow and Glasgow Jock to send on a baler and a combine instead.

Season of the Champions

Our upland year has moved into its magnificent finale. The season of the great calf sales is upon us and every farm worth its rugged acres can think of nothing, talk of nothing, but the champions and prices of last week's events, the prospects and rewards of next week's round.

Farmers scurrying from mart to mart beneath the lowering backend skies note the splintered rainbows littering the horizon and the great gulls riding in from storm on the firth, and turn up the collars of their coats against the smell of bitter weather. But their precaution is no more than a gesture towards the inclement time. Intent on their catalogues and pens of calves, they feel neither cold nor mud nor even dinner hour long past.

Not all calf sales by a long chalk take place in our heightened atmosphere. In most of Britain they occur in the hum-drum of agricultural business. But then the people who deal there are interested only in the paper pattern calf – the norm the supermarket ultimately demands.

We for our part admit such conditions do exist, but we refuse to be bound by their mundane exigencies. We care not for the norm; what we strive for is the ideal; that calf whose breeding, conformation, and firm fleshiness exists with Plato's table in the unattainable infinite.

With such a virtuoso outlook it might be thought that only super specialists would attend our calf sales. Not a bit of it. Everybody, and I mean just that, turns up to appraise, weigh, adjudicate, and argue. Some sales pull in bigger audiences than others, but probably the greatest draw is Grantown, where the great calf festival opens in the third week in September. Indeed, so great is the press of onlookers there that the legitimate buyers and sellers find difficulty in moving round to do business.

It says much for the atmosphere of the place that no one registers any very vocal complaint about conditions which are comfortless to a degree as well as being inconvenient. Anyway with the Cairngorms standing around grooming themselves for another smashing winter sporting season, and dramatic recollections of the chap who paid 500 quid for a calf at the show here a month ago, who cares for obstructing crush – except, maybe, the calves?

The sale begins after the judging of the prize-winners. Like a conductor of an orchestra the auctioneer mounts the rostrum and at once the buyers raise their instruments; hands, catalogues, or merely eyebrows. Against the steady drum of the auctioneer's recap of bids the theme sways back and forth. The entertainment will last for hours. But at last it is over; the last bid indicated, the last cathartic cheque signed.

Only whispers remain in the now quiet ring – arcana of calf rearing which by tomorrow will have assumed the stature of legend.

The Five Cats in the Barn

There are only five cats living in the barn now; a sad comedown from the days when more than double that number spent their velvet hours hunting the mice who infiltrated from their winter quarters in the corn stacks standing foursquare against hungry winter on an upland moor.

In those piping times of unquestioned M.A.P. aid we pursued a different type of farming from that we follow today. Then the byre was full of milk cows and the folds full of cogged calves. Now the cows are out on the hill, looking after their calves themselves; and we who used to enjoy the prodigality of milk by the pail must now count out its parsimony by the pint. In place of stacks in the yard there are polythene-sheeted silage pits by the Dutch barn.

* * *

The cats who are still with us, however, do not seem to spend useless regrets for a specious past. Indeed they have taken quite kindly to the tin of vitamin-enforced cat food in place of the wooden bowls of warm, foaming milk that was their staple diet.

They hunt mice still, and keep themselves in training by walking the rafters above the empty stalls in the deserted byres. Impervious or philosophic, none of them has complained about their altered lot. That is none except Smiler, a plain little black and white feline with no front teeth.

Three years ago Smiler decided that the rugged life in outhouse and loft was not for her. She made up her mind to move in with the humans. They protested loudly but she was adamant, pointing out that her habits were cleanly to the point of immaculacy. We capitulated. She came to stay.

* * *

During the time she has lived with us she has been so successful in bending us to her will that we hardly dare answer the telephone without inviting her to come and listen. When I type she sits on the desk in a sunny spot and comments frankly on the hunt and pick efforts of the amateur. Bored, waiting for me to finish, she scans the bookshelves, throwing out the volumes she deems unsuitable for me to read. When the last letter is written and the last stamp licked she bounds joyfully to the door.

Shall we go and clean the potatoes? Shall we take a walk in the wood? Not that she likes getting her feet wet but she wants once more to try to show me how to bound from boulder to tussock in a graceful dry-shod way. "Clumsy," she whistles through her toothless gums when I splatter.

She talks all the time. Did I see the grouse? The pheasants in the wild wet trees? There is the butcher's van; the last mince was too fatty; the collie has not been shut in; she has not been introduced to the new postman. At last, night comes and with it the armchair, the fire, and her two humans. Voluptuously she stretches this way and that, while far down in her throat she purrs contentedly, musing happily on a cat's life.

Lemon for the Willow

Summer's crowding traffic is at last perceptibly thinning on our country roads. The second-last bus full of R.A.F. personnel on leave has climbed the long hill from the coast on its way south; the last cockle shell of a holiday caravan has titupped protestingly on its draw bar, home to winter quarters.

No more Sunday afternoon excursions for the motorist from the Laich, anxious to spend the odd sunshiny hour by moor and the sandy bays that margin Lochindorb. In a week or so the big commercial vans and trucks which increasingly carry all our merchandise will, save for the antrin farm tractor scurrying from field to steading, have the road all to themselves.

The wind blows continuously now, bawling and banging in the steading and threatening stacks and sheeted silage pits. The rowan tree has been stripped of every leaf, but its blood-bright berries still shine out radiantly, demolishing the centuries and making the observer companion to the Anglo-Saxon poet who saw this self-same sight before he wrote his Holy Rood, the holy tree that was the Cross.

* * *

October brings scarlet for the gean and lemon for the willow, fountaining above the wooden hut that simultaneously provides shelter for the rural traveller waiting for the bus and the pints of milk left by a trusting Milk Marketeer to be collected by appropriate owners.

Contractors' combines still clutter farm closes. If they were not such Frankensteinish clunks of machinery, one would say they were straining at the leash. They spend every opportune moment in the battered fields salvaging a crop that away back in July looked like being memorable. In the 10 good days September afforded us, a great deal of harvesting was accomplished but there remains much to do and it must be drudged through somehow.

When the last bag of corn – no matter what its moisture content – comes off the trailer, the farmer is too relieved to see it to take much notice of the untidy chewed stubble that remains. Perhaps a winter keep scheme which compels us into crops other than cereal will not be without its advantages. The weather certainly looks like coming down on the side of the departmental battalions.

Cattle beasts in the fields consider sending a deputation to the farmer inquiring about the possibility of extra rations in the near future. The farmer does a rapid sum which he hopes will give him the answer to how many mouths he can support on the place till the spring.

While he struggles to equate cows to silage and sheep to hay, the geese go tangling down the gale; children get ready to dook for apples, and witches with their eye on Halloween look out fresh broomsticks for their coven. Wyvis across the western firth wears a premonition of snow about his brow and along with winter regards us all.

Annals in the "Cottage" Cupboard

Every so often I take in hand with the "Cottage" cupboard where the debris of three generations has been accumulated. "The Cottage" is the name we give the house built by my great-grandmother. When her husband, who farmed outside Inverness, died she came to live in Nairn, where with financial help from her two elder sons she built her "cottage".

In the middle of last century when space was no object a house with only two storeys and with dressing-rooms for but two of its bedrooms would have been regarded as a cottage. Great-grandma, invested with the divine right of matriarchy and black satin called it so, and we have obediently followed her edict.

The cupboard had been coped with by previous generations and by my time was inhabited chiefly by photographs of Victorian relatives and hideous amateur watercolours of Egyptian scenes. For seven years I have been burning and dumping; then last week I decided on a final sweep down to the ultimate colossal cruet and the final Brown's Bible.

There must be hundreds of cottage cupboards like mine in Scotland, stacked with the annals of those country folk who retired to pleasant little county towns where life is singularly unlike that depicted in our more melodramatic native novels, and where people lead dignified lives in comfortable decorum.

Perhaps only in the faces of my stiffly photographed ancestors could be glimpsed the character which gives Scots their peculiar demon. There was for instance that group of Japanese business associates all wearing snazzy kimonos and making a background for my great-uncles looking exactly what they were, Scots country lads on the blatant up and up. At one time they made fortunes out of China tea, but owing to pig-headedness lost most of it when Indian tea took its popular place in world markets.

Other forbears lived less exotic lives. With their high cheek bones and uncompromising mouths their prototypes can be seen anywhere is northern Scotland today – at mart or Kirk. In their day they took a suitable interest in the ministers of their religion, as witness the lithograph of Dr Macdonald, the Apostle of the North, bland faced as an egg looking out of the spotless cup of a white cravat. It was apt that such a well-nourished divine should be found reposing above the family cookery book.

This book writ in a number of fair Italian hands began in 1818 with a recipe for Cherry Brandy. Recipes were collected till 1872, but not all by the same ancestor. They were, however, similarly animated by ideas which make the convention of Scots thrift look silly. Eighteen eggs went into a sponge cake while brandy flowed by the quart. Each recipe is dated and accredited to its source. "A gentleman from the North" is responsible for a potent ginger cordial, while an anonymous Quaker contributes an equally spirituous currant wine. Not all the entries are for food. Some are for general household use. Of these my favourite, dated 6th September, 1830, is for Preserving Roses for Winter Use. It has a dying fall apposite to autumnal days.

Non-Co-operative Account

Twenty years ago farm accounting existed on two levels, A and O. In A the farmer used the back of any handy envelope to work out how much he had to spend to keep his enterprise going; how much he was likely to receive for his produce. Receipts-Expenses-Income. Q.E.D.

O level, though it entailed less homework, engendered more emotion; but then its noble simplicity could not be denied. The farmer merely entered the bank on mart day and inquired in the immortal words of a neighbour of mine "Am I overdriven?"

However convenient each method appeared to him who practiced it, neither was acceptable to the Inland Revenue. In spite of protests farmers were herded into the accountants' offices, there to be sold ledgers labelled Farm Accounts which not only had to be kept up to date but had to be exposed to the indecent scrutiny of the Income Taxers. Considering the traditional conservativeness of agriculture it was wonderful how quickly farmers learned the habit of preserving cheque stubs as well as the art of matching mart receipts to movement of stock records.

Then just as the industry was congratulating itself on its modern business methods, its own blood pundits turned on it and demanded that it look again to its accountancy. Rugged individualism was out – farm co-operatives were in. Buy in bulk and avoid bankruptcy was the forward-sounding slogan. The result of all this has been that farming, especially in the South, has come out in a rash of co-operative marketing groups dealing in feeding stuff, grain, fertiliser, calves, the lot.

Not wishing to be all that backwoods in this brave new world we had a meeting ourselves the other week to listen to the gospel according to co-operation. As we listened we realised that all unbeknown to ourselves we had been co-operating for years. True, we had done it unaware while Sammy, the contractor we employ to take our beasts to and from the market, had organised the journeys to suit both him and us. Nor had we tumbled to it that Donny, who does our agricultural contracting, had been streamlining our silage making, our combine harvesting, and our hay bailing. Nothing could have been neater nor more efficient than the dovetailing in which we'd been unconsciously participating.

In an odd way we were gratified, but no one likes to have their ego deflated however just the cause, so when the further proposition came of going farther along the road of co-operation and buying in bulk among fellow farmers we turned obstinate. Forgo, besides, the delicious manoeuvres which fill the wastes of many a wintry afternoon when discounts are seen to be wrung from the representatives of the firms with whom we deal? Forgo, too, the triumphant *quid pro quo* of, you buy my corn, I buy your fertiliser? Forgo the shrewd blackmailing of no draff, no order for grass seed? Not Doolittle likely. We keep our non co-operative account.

Weather to Measure

To the delight of farmers and the dismay of ski-lifters November has gone all bland on us. Not a trace of last week's snow lurks in the lythe behind the sun, while through the vaporous thaw half obscuring the firth the great peaks float in vague benignant blue.

The sheep are gone to the hill and the outwintering cows forage happily in the rough. It is as delightful as surprising, but one wonders whether the weather clerk's arrangement of the matter has not been motivated by a Puckish desire to cut down to size those Met. men who have been sticking out their necks by promising weather, if not to measure, at least ready-made.

Some southern contemporaries are sceptical about long-range weather wisdom; but we who live in the flat above the R.A.F. at Kinloss ruefully remember the horrid accuracy of their Met. office's predictions over the past two years and are prepared to grant them expertise if not second sight.

Of course before the Air Ministry took over the lands by the ancient abbey we had our own rule of thumb methods of foretelling the weather. It was but natural that country people whose living depended so much on the elements should study their vagaries. Across the centuries such observations were distilled into the rustic verses we still quote and more than half believe. "Mony haws mak' mony snaws," we say, acknowledging not only the onset of winter but also dimly recognising the Creator's benevolence towards his birds by spreading an unusual profusion of berries along the hedgerows to sustain them through the hungry months to come.

In the Scottish folk calendar each month has its appropriate lore. Of the 12, February is most fully documented. Here we are fond of the Candlemas rhyme which falls for repetition on the second of that month and commemorates the festival for the purification of the Virgin:

If Candlemas Day be dry and fair
The half of winter's to come and mair.
If Candlemas Day be wet and foul
The half of winter's by at Yule.

This jingle is Doric for the Latin distich once general to much of Europe.

Si sol splendecat Maria Purificante
Major erit glacies post festum quam ante.

But however impressive such vaticinations sound, country folk pay their real credence to the behaviour of the birds and beasts who share the world with them. Cows gambolling clumsily in the field foretell heavy rain. Navigating gulls steering inland by the rivers are sailing in the front of tempest; while the storm cock clinging to his rigging in the larch shouting melodious defiance against the morning mirk assures us of wild weather lying in wait the day beyond tomorrow. We have never known him wrong.

Towards the Solstice

When the last batch of calves is sold and the December returns filled in and sent on their way to Edinburgh, we feel we can permit ourselves an anticipatory thought for the winter solstice that blessed moment a mere fortnight away, when the sun must perforce turn on his heel to begin his return journey to a reviving year.

The long drag of November is behind us and though the end of January, when the difference in daylight will be really obvious, is still far away, the thought that "woeful winter's weary waste" is half gone is encouraging.

Winter anywhere in the Scottish countryside lacks style, but winter in the saucer of an upland moor is plain dull and lacklustre. This is a district that needs sunlight to give it meaning; without it our aesthetic of freedom beyond the untrammelled horizon does not exist. In the short reluctant day the folding acre upon acre of withered heather and dun hill grass filch what little light there is. When a pale sun puts out an apologetic beam the serried conifers, cohorts of claustrophobia, marching densely south and west plunder whatever glimmer Dava has not already absorbed. Abandoned by the sun, not yet encompassed by the night we inhabit a nether world of in between.

* * *

Lank, dispirited silence lies about us. The cheerful bustling noises of other seasons are vanished. The listener eager for a companionable whisper resigns himself to the sound of wintering sheep pattering on their silly little cardboard hooves across the tarmac dividing field from hill. For a change he can hear the cattle slowly squelching through the mud between barn and court. The little birds with whom we loved to pass the time of day have either gone from here or retreated to mute thickets. True, we have the robin, and the storm cock, one on the fence, the other in the larch; but they communicate only at intervals and then to announce the imminence of storm and snow. Occasionally a neighbour starts up his power-saw in the birch woods by the river. The high whine startles the grouse quietly feeding in the park nearest the house. Hurriedly recollecting their vows to abjure "vineyard, field, and seed," they make off like the Rechabite to the tents of the wilderness and silence resumes its habit.

All times of the year have their appropriate scents and winter has its acrid comment on the hour. From newly opened silage pit comes the sweetish sourish smell of ensiled grass familiar enough in a district that knows the reek of distillery effluent. Happily the cattle have no reservations about the appetising qualities of self-feed fare. All they want is to get there before Frees beats them to it. Frees is an enormous black and white stot we keep more for the sake of inquiring interest than for financial gain. We long to know when he will stop growing and when his colossal appetite will become jaded. So far his joyful gluttony offers no answer to either question.

Sheets (Balance) in the Wind

Annual general meetings with their accompanying balance-sheets are never popular in our part of the world, especially with the committee members who are not accorded the dispensation which allows the general public to operate *in absenita.*

Who wants to spend the draughty winter hour arguing the toss in the hall when criticism can be so much more trenchant – and comfortable – by one's own fireside in the company of the dambrod, the telly, and the dram?

Perhaps this is why the secretary of our village hall, relying on the season of good will, has summoned us to a hall meeting on a date as near Christmas as possible. I doubt if her thought will either encourage the public at large to do their attendance duty or affect the more recalcitrant committee members with a rush of peaceability.

Audits in the country can be relied on to produce their miasma of peculiar gloom and ours is no exception save that it operates in reverse. Most village activities are as poor as proverbial mice, but we – we have money in the bank. Lots of it.

Over the years we have accrued a respectable balance in order to modernise our tiny timber-built hall. At long last we are ready to go ahead and have even got our plan drawn up. But now we wonder if there are going to be enough people left in the glen to take advantage of our new Stak-a-By chairs and the revolutionised cloakrooms.

We have lived so long with the rural depopulating process we hardly notice our decay unless something dramatic like the closing of our country schools brings it home to our painful bosoms. We had barely recovered from our educational streamlining when we were confronted with the fact that we may lose our railway in the near future. Therefore we must take a long, cool look at our condition.

If the station goes we shall have no real heart left in the district, for the nine or ten families in the cluster of houses in the cutting are the nucleus that binds us together and gives us shape. The farmhouses dotted over the acres of intervening moor are a monument to our ability to come to terms with solitude rather than the epitome of cheerful communal living.

At first, March was fixed for our execution but now the evil day is postponed. We wish "MacPuff" every success in his endeavours but we have been so conditioned to merciless administrative convenience so long that we are not buoyed up any false hope and are resigned to seeing Dava take over to its heathery embrace the stretch of track between Forres and Grantown.

So here we are with money to lush up our hall and hardly anybody left to enjoy its amenity. That our predicament is vexatious there is no gainsaying; that a wry humour attaches to our embarrassingly favourable balance-sheet is undeniable; that the committee's instinct is to hang it with two other sheets in the wind before going on the spree themselves is understandable.

"The Daft Days"
- Modern Style

The workmen who are excavating new tracks for the telephone system by the side of our steeply meandering hill road are working like beavers to get as much done as possible before Hogmanay, when they'll relax for that midwinter festival so peculiarly congenial to the outrageous Scottish heart.

There has always been a day or two's respite at this time, and with less Spartan ideas gaining popularity, these days – the Daft Days of our ancestors – look like establishing themselves firmly as a general holiday for everyone.

Since time immemorial the favourite recreation of the season was "the shoot." It was and is a masculine preserve which age does not wither nor custom stale its singular lack of variety. At every road confluence there is an untidy huddle of those husky cars popular with lairds and gamekeepers.

Tall men, their complexions reddened with the cold, their eyes glittering with excitement, stand tensely in the coverts where the river sweeps by precipitous banks crowned with noble oaks and beeches. Gun dogs, impervious to the exasperation and screaming brakes of other road users, flush and retrieve with the suave purpose of the highly trained professional. The scene is full of harsh wild beauty.

There can be no more lively way of spending the short, bright northern day than in enjoying the dry, clean wind wrinkling in the dead leaves still clinging to the deciduous trees, waiting for it to subside before the frost that comes to kindle its incandescence in the sky, expectant for the rush and soar of jewelled birds.

The crystal hills stand listening for the echoes that will ultimately die along their snowy hearts. If each man kills the thing he loves, the strange paradox where death and loveliness are inextricable is for once resolved.

Luckily for those less committed to complication our countryside provides simpler enjoyments. The cars streaming past with passengers packed inside and skis strapped outside are on their way to the slopes in the Cairngorms where Norwegians, Austrians, and Swiss encourage us to enjoy the pleasures inherent in our own mountains. The winter season opened officially on the week-end before Christmas with new hotels making glossy news and old ones keeping up valiantly.

The original inhabitants are not quite sure what to make of their Cinderella transformation from hillbillies to soignés sophisticates. Naturally we realise the magnitude of the match we have made with the Fairy Prince of Tourism. But we have our moments when we yearn to throw off our glass slippers and put on our comfortable old bauchles as we toast our toes before a messy, inefficient but oh so homely, peat fire. But there is no return.

Anyway we are learning to appreciate our central heating, our fitted carpets, and our flower decorations à la Constance Spry. In no time at all we shall have our old daft days smoothly integrated into an expanding winter sporting season.

4th January - 1964

Getting Around

Like most of our country neighbours whose townee children make a beeline for the old farmstead during the winter holiday, we are recovering our breath after meeting our young and despatching them, after a few days, back to the scene of their endeavours.

When we were not motoring to an airport to collect one daughter, we were hurling down to a railway station to salvage another. We found the trains better at keeping to their timetables than the aeroplanes, and the buses better than either. But that element of improvisation essential to travel in the uncharted north was in evidence all the time.

When the telephone rang at an unearthly hour to allow a breathless voice to announce its owner's arrival at an unforeseen destination we took it matter-of-factly. Not for nothing do I remember the old Highlander I met long ago outside the B.B.C. studios in Edinburgh. He had had to make a long complicated journey to get there, and on being congratulated on his timeous arrival remarked: - "Ach, if I had taken the train I didn't take, I wouldn't have been here yet."

* * *

Actually we are slick at getting around in our part of the world. It is an old Moravian custom dating back to the days when we lay on a suitable route for avenging armies and marauding Highlanders.

In these circumstances it paid to know one's way about as Sir Andrew Moray understood in 1336. He had been besieging Lochindorb Castle where the Countess of Athole – "with uther ladyis that ware luvly" – was seeking safety. Unable to reduce the stronghold he retreated towards the firth with Edward III in pursuit. Sir Andrew's progress was leisurely and he took his time before camping in Altyre woods by the river Findhorn at its most turbulent.

The enemy supposed that by making a proper dispensation of troops they could cut off Sir Andrew's retreat south and west with the river doing the same for the north and east. The sturdy old gentleman, none put out, retired to his tent where he observed the tenets of the proverb which observes that prayer and provender never hindered any man. On emerging he serenely repaired an armour strap and then coolly led his troops down "a byway that ewyn down betwixt crags lay through that strayte rode." When the English appeared the Scots had gone.

Because we continued to be clever wayfarers over the years, we worked out a neat convenient way on which to drive our cattle to the old trysts and fairs at Falkirk. That old road is still visible in the heather of our rough grazing and the farms that fringed its path ring their triple syllabled names sweetly in memory's ear.

The railway follows the disused highway. Soon we expect that to fall into desuetude also.

Industry in the Wild

The recent announcement about a new look for the Scottish Country Industries Development Trust must have a special interest for those of us who were in on the ground floor of the undertaking.

In 1936 Scotland was one huge depressed area and by way of acknowledging our plight the Government decided to investigate the condition of our country trades. The three south-western counties, Dumfries, Kirkcudbright, and Wigtown were selected for the initial survey and the project was put under the cosy grandmotherly wing of Highland Home Industries.

To people newly come from feudal Highland fastnesses the lives and habits of the natives of the South-West were not only refreshing but exhilarating; in contrast to the sweet smooth green of the scenery the inhabitants were rugged people of independent minds and inventive genius. Like their Norse forebears, they were tall, blue-eyed, and golden-haired and they faced life with forthright resilience.

At this time the great mechanical revolution in farming was beginning and every country smiddy and carpenter's shop had already evolved its answer to the changing methods. Indeed, so many were the fertile minds and engineering capabilities that *The Glasgow Herald* published an article on the subject which the then director of education in Dumfries asked permission to republish so that he might distribute it through the schools in his county.

* * *

What clearly emerged from the survey was that though a regrettably large number of country workshops had packed up, those that remained were run by men of adventure and imaginative shrewdness. They realised they needed help, but the aid they required was, alas, not that which Highland Home Industries was able to give nor indeed envisage.

The wrights, smiths, and agricultural engineers were for none of that competent church bazaar aura which did very well with the Highland enterprise; still less did they want any truck with Ye Olde Celtic Twilight which, though it might be a strong selling suit with ancient tartan setts and crofter carved driftwood, meant nothing in industries already seeing their future bound up in things like improved costing, general business method, and the finer points of acetylene welding.

The painful dichotomy was further exacerbated by a connection with the English Rural Bureau, which had been for years successful with English country crafts and which therefore had to be regarded as the sole arbiter of taste and oracle of advice. The smiths in the South-West were for none of the wrought-iron inn signs and other frivolous products of the English. What they wanted was an extramural course conducted by Anderson's of Glasgow. Their remarks anent some of the more genteel do-goodery suggested to them were worthy of their eminent cousin from Ecclefechan.

Now presumably all this is old history; and judging from the names and the new charter, S.C.I.D.T. is all set for less nerve-wracked days and more professional standards. Their countrymen wish them all the luck they'll need.

Co-operative Weather

Although winter achieves its solstice by December 22 there seems no appreciable difference in the returning light till the end of January. True the day does appear to linger into evening; but the mornings remain reluctant to show face.

When, as is generally our case, we are wading in drift all through the month, alternately placating St Agnes with her "hare leaping trembling through the frozen grass," or St Hilary, whose January feast day is supposed to be the coldest day of the year, we are glad to take advantage of the dark to lie comfortably abed. But 1964, in contrast to its two stormy predecessors, has turned out balmy – not comparatively balmy – but balmy enough to take out the lawn mower and marvel at the shoots sent out by roses heeled in in December.

The unseasonably co-operative temperature has presented the hill farmer with a pretty dilemma. Normally he goes round wailing about ploughing still undone. Now he has no snow, no frost; working conditions are ideal and every prospect would please if only economic conditions did not look so vile.

The coming year is so fraught with the twin anxieties of Winter Keep and Standard Quantities that everyone is doubtful whether hallowed farming practice is going to pay off or land us all in bankruptcy.

Winter Keep, which affects only the hill farmer, means a change in his cropping. Instead of growing cereals for cash he must grow them for feeding to his beasts. In return he will get Government assistance to help him to grow suitable winter keep. Standard Quantities means an agricultural *quid pro quo* which will exchange a restriction in subsidised cropping for a degree of control in imported food.

Of the two measures the second seems to arouse more angry misgiving here, though it might have been supposed that in an upland district the other scheme would have come home more to our hearts and bosoms. Perhaps it was because the implications of Standard Quantities burst on us just as the country was running its Freedom from Hunger campaign that we are so incensed. It was a protest against the cockeyed, and not niggardly, parochialism that insisted that the proceeds from the children's nativity play should not go entirely to the starving but should help the school fund as well.

Meanwhile, heedless of world conditions, the beasts of the field and wild enjoy the time with happy thoughtlessness. The first of the new season's calves take the air with their decorous mothers on the way to the self-feed silage pit. The expensive gadget we bought to cope with slurry consequent on blizzard and blast has not had a chance yet to show its potentialities; neither has the sludge pit excavated with much boulderish difficulty.

But we bear up. We are content to view the hills across the firth snowless, scarfed in sunlight. Every hill corry is loud with the bravado of the cock grouse, while five starlings laugh infectiously in the larch tree. The fox, deep in the hidden wood, smiles to think how well he can conceal his tracks and the white hare out on the moor wonders if the platinum blonde stuff should be overdone this season.

Morn, when at last it comes, wears a smudged caress of cloud across its forehead and the aconites, brave little Atlases, bear the burden of winter blithely on thrusting golden shoulders.

Books, Bed and Board

Until the Robbins Report no one in our heights took much interest in the agitation for a sixth university. This is surprising because one of our main exports for years has been brains.

Till now we have taken it for granted that the universities to which we owe ancient allegiance would accept our children as students. Entrance qualifications did not bother us unduly for our teaching tradition sees to it that our pupils are pretty well found in that respect.

But none of us had ever visualised the physical horrors of classrooms so jammed with students that professors and lecturers have to battle a way to the rostrum. We cannot any longer gainsay the necessity for another university.

So we look around to consider the claims of those towns so anxious to provide a new site. They have all done admirable homework before presenting their cases. No one can deny the excellence of their briefs even while suspecting they want the sixth for the sake of industrial prestige rather than for pure learning. But to the Highlander, all the claimants but one fall down on the same thing – the question of student residences. Where are the milling scholars to live? The great trump card Inverness holds is that it has already the nucleus of a residential quarter.

Unlike the more heavily populated parts we in the North have long been used to the idea of the studying young leaving home. Living away from the parental roof has enabled our students to absorb some degree of that worldly wisdom so noticeably lacking in the academics whose mothers do their washing for them as well as making their meals and beds for them.

Central Scotland must realise that study at a university means going away from home. This merciful compulsion on the Highland student was the origin of the great tradition of the Aberdeen landlady – that dynamic personality who warmed and admonished her lodgers so successfully that on graduation day she was the first to receive one of the prized invitation cards for the ceremony.

Which Aberdeen graduate has not his own private recollection of his landlady commenting as shrewdly on his books and professors as on his own shortcomings?

Today the landlady of that old school still exists but not in nearly sufficient numbers and the waxing student body finds itself without living accommodation or even a roof under which to read a textbook. With the influx of foreign students on top of our own bulge the difficulty gets more intolerable every term.

It is some years now since Aberdeen with its high proportion of non-native students realised what was happening and with a lucky inheritance was able to build the first residential hall in Britain to house both men and women students. Now they are rushing to convert big houses in the precinct into quarters for more scholars, while the new generations clamour to get in before the plaster is dry or the painters have begun.

No wonder then that those of us uncomfortably close to the problem opt every time for Inverness with its offer of ready-made lodgings in addition to its other advantages. In the event of my living to see my grandchildren going there instead of to Aberdeen I hope I shall remember having written this and not yearn too painfully after an Alma Mater who cannot accommodate my descendants.